The Jewish Background

of the

CHRISTIAN LITURGY

74890

The Jewish Background

of the

CHRISTIAN LITURGY

by

W. O. E. OESTERLEY, D.D.

Rector of St. Mary Aldermary, E.C. 4
Examining Chaplain to the Bishop of London

OXFORD
AT THE CLARENDON PRESS
1925

Oxford University Press

London   Edinburgh   Glasgow   Copenhagen
New York   Toronto   Melbourne   Cape Town
Bombay   Calcutta   Madras   Shanghai
Humphrey Milford Publisher to the UNIVERSITY

Printed in England

PREFACE

THE object of this volume is to show that the Jewish Liturgy has left many marks of its influence, both in thought and word, on early forms of Christian worship, and, therefore, ultimately on the Christian Liturgy itself. The truth of this is acknowledged, in a general way, by all liturgiologists; but the aim of the present writer is to give definite details and illustrations of this on a fairly comprehensive scale.

The task involves, of course, as a preliminary, a careful study of the Jewish Liturgy. But that is only the first step. That Liturgy in all its extant forms contains a great mass of material belonging to times subsequent to the beginning of the Christian era. What we require to know, however, are the pre-Christian elements in the Jewish Liturgy, for it is obviously only these elements that can come into consideration in seeking to show in what respects Jewish influence has left its marks on early Christian forms of worship.

To determine what portions of the Jewish Liturgy are pre-Christian is by no means always an easy matter; in some cases, it is true, there is no difficulty at all; but in what is, in some respects, the most important domain of all, viz. forms of prayer, great care is needed, and a variety of factors have to be taken into consideration. It is to be expected that the views of authoritative Jewish liturgiologists should differ in some cases as to the date of some particular portion of the Liturgy; but with only a few exceptions the bulk of expert opinion is agreed as to the pre-Christian portions; differences of opinion deal rather with dates within the pre- or post-Christian era respectively. In Chapter II, which is concerned with this part of our subject, we give our reasons for regarding as pre-Christian those elements which come into consideration; so that the reader can judge for himself whether our contention is justified or not.

In connexion with the Jewish Liturgy we have to face at the outset an objection which requires to be dealt with before we can enter upon our task. The sources for our knowledge of the early history of the Jewish Liturgy belong for the most part, in their present form, to Christian times. It will, therefore, be asked how these sources can be regarded as reliable for our present purpose. This important subject is dealt with in the opening chapter, where reasons, which it is hoped will be regarded as adequate, are given to show that these sources are reliable.

In the second chapter the Jewish Liturgy, so far as its pre-Christian elements are concerned, is considered. These two chapters constitute Part I.

We come then to the early forms of Christian worship. In the investigations undertaken both in this Part and in Part III it is so important that the religious environment of the first generation or two of Christians should be borne in mind that a short chapter (III) is devoted to the subject of the worship of the early Christian communities. It is fully realized that the ground covered in this chapter is very familiar; but the writer craves the forbearance of his readers, who will recognize, he feels sure, how necessary it is to get into the religious atmosphere of New Testament times if justice is to be done to the general subject of the book.

Chapter IV contains a brief enumeration of the sources for the earliest forms of Christian worship.

With Chapter V we enter upon the essence of our task, the endeavour being made, by means of a number of illustrations, to show in what respects early forms of Christian worship were influenced by the Jewish Liturgy. It will be conceded, we believe, that in most of the illustrations given Jewish influence is indubitable ; in some cases this influence may not be immediately apparent, but closer scrutiny will, we are convinced, reveal it.

Part III is a continuation of these illustrations in the form of special studies, though in these it is not so much the Jewish Liturgy as the general Jewish background that is laid under contribution. The first of these special studies deals with the antecedents of the Eucharist. The subject is an intricate one, and the theory advocated runs counter to the traditional belief that the Eucharist was instituted at a Passover meal. As will be pointed out, the theory in itself is not new ; but as hitherto presented it contains some flaws. The present writer has some new arguments to offer which, he believes, eliminates these flaws.

There follows then a study on the origin of the *Agapé* which has some points of attachment with the preceding one. A new theory of its origin is propounded, which, though only of antiquarian importance, will, it is hoped, not be without interest.

The concluding study is concerned with the origin of the *Epiclesis* ; and here again a new theory is put forward which may be of some interest in view of the controversy at the present time on the subject of the *Epiclesis*.

. . . .

Both Greek, and especially Hebrew, type has been avoided as far as possible; but here and there, for one reason or another, Greek, much more rarely Hebrew, type occurs.

. . . .

Originally my old and valued friend, Canon Box, intended to collaborate with me in this work, as we have so happily done in the case of several books previously. But he found the pressure of other work too great, and had reluctantly to give up his original intention. This has been a matter of real regret to both of us; but especially to me, for his collaboration would have greatly enhanced whatever value the book may have. He has, however, been kind enough to read through a considerable part of my manuscript, so that I believe there is little, if anything, in the following pages with which he is not in substantial agreement.

I desire to express my warmest thanks to the Secretary of the Clarendon Press for his unfailing kindness and courtesy.

W. O. E. OESTERLEY.

CONTENTS

PART I. THE JEWISH LITURGY

I

RELIABILITY OF THE SOURCES

II

THE PRE-CHRISTIAN ELEMENTS IN THE JEWISH LITURGY

PART II. *JEWISH LITURGICAL INFLUENCE ON EARLY FORMS OF CHRISTIAN WORSHIP*

III

WORSHIP IN THE EARLY CHRISTIAN COMMUNITIES

IV

SOURCES FOR THE EARLIEST FORMS OF CHRISTIAN WORSHIP

Contents

V

THE INFLUENCE OF THE JEWISH LITURGY ON EARLY FORMS OF CHRISTIAN WORSHIP

PART III. SPECIAL STUDIES

VI

THE ANTECEDENTS OF THE EUCHARIST

VII

FURTHER ARGUMENTS IN SUPPORT OF THE THEORY ADVOCATED IN THE PRECEDING CHAPTER

Contents

VIII

THE ORIGIN OF THE *AGAPÉ*

IX

THE ORIGIN OF THE *EPICLESIS*

INDEXES

ABBREVIATIONS

BT The Babylonian Talmud.

ERE Hastings' *Encyclopaedia of Religion and Ethics.*

JE The Jewish Encyclopaedia.

JQR The Jewish Quarterly Review.

JTS The Journal of Theological Studies.

*RWS*² *The Religion and Worship of the Synagogue* (2nd ed., 1911), by Oesterley and Box.

SLRJ *A Short Survey of the Literature of Rabbinical and Mediaeval Judaism* (1920), by Oesterley and Box.

Elbogen, *Der jüdische Gottesdienst in seiner geschichtlichen Entwicklung* (1913).

Zunz, *Die gottesdienstlichen Vorträge der Juden, historisch entwickelt* (1892).

PART I
THE JEWISH LITURGY

I

RELIABILITY OF THE SOURCES

In seeking to show in what respects early forms of Christian worship were influenced by the Jewish Liturgy, it is, of course, necessary to indicate *what* elements in the latter are believed to have left their impress on the former. It is necessary to show, further, that these elements in the Jewish Liturgy are, or at any rate were in their original form, pre-Christian. But inasmuch as most of our information regarding the early forms of Jewish worship is gained from the Mishnah primarily, though also from the Tosephta, the Gemara, and the earlier Midrashim,—and inasmuch as it may well be asked whether we are justified in utilizing these post-Christian documents for establishing our contention, and whether the traditions they contain on the subject are reliable,—it must be a preliminary task to set forth the reasons why we are justified in using these documents for the purpose, and why the traditions contained in them may be regarded as reliable.

It is not claimed that irrefutable proofs can be adduced; but it can be shown, we submit, that the facts of the case are such as to make it reasonably probable that, generally speaking, and so far at any rate as liturgical *data* are concerned, the statements gathered from this body of literature may be accepted as reliable.

As we have said, our principal authorities for this purpose are the Mishnah, the Tosephta, and the Gemara, to which may be added the earlier Midrashim. In many respects the most important of these authorities are the Mishnah and the Tosephta. The latter often affords interesting and valuable evidence which is not to be found in the Mishnah; indeed, one can go so far as to say that the Tosephta may be regarded as a parallel authority to the Mishnah itself; and, in fact, just because it does not possess the official authority attaching to the Mishnah text, it is often for this very reason *more* valuable in preserving *data* that were deliberately rejected from the official authority, and would otherwise have been lost. For sometimes opinions and points of view are referred to which did not harmonize with the *ultimately* accepted authoritative rule; these are largely represented in the Tosephta. Another valuable element is the frequent illustration of a rule or practice by some specific instance narrated, in many cases, in the form of a story; these concrete illustrations preserved in the Tosephta are often highly illuminating.[1]

Regarding the question of the dates in general of these several bodies of literature, a clear and concise statement of fact is given by Abelson. As to the Talmud (i.e. Mishnah and Gemara; the Tosephta can be included under the former, so far as date is concerned), the earliest date associated with it

'is that of the pre-Tannaites or *Zekēnim Ha-Reshônim* [i. e. the Earlier Elders], starting with Antigonus of Socho, who flourished about the first half of the third

---

[1] See, further, Elbogen's valuable article, ' Bemerkungen zur alten jüdischen Liturgie ', in *Studies in Jewish Literature in honour of K. Kohler*, pp. 74–81 (1913).

century B. C., and was, according to the Mishnah
(*Aboth* i), the disciple and successor of Simon the
Just. The last of these were Hillel and Shammai.
Following on the demise of these, there commenced
the period of the Tannaim [i.e. Teachers], lasting from
the commencement of the Christian era until about the
first quarter of the third century A. D. ; Hillel and
Shammai belong to the last pre-Christian century. . . .
With them, and the band of Tannaim that succeeded
to their teachings, the Talmudic age proper may be
said to have commenced. Hence the *terminus a quo*
of Talmudic literature must be assigned roughly to
the opening years of the first Christian century. The
terminus ad quem is the close of the epoch of the
Saboraim [i.e. Explainers], which, according to the
famous letter of R. Sherira (edit. Neubauer in *Mediaeval
Jewish Chronicles*, i. 180), would be toward the end of
the second half of the sixth century.' [1]

It is, then, from about 250 B. C. onwards that the
material, embedded in which our evidence is to be
sought, was in process of growth ; and this evidence
exists by no means only in the later centuries of this
long period ; for from its beginning ' stores of accumu-
lated learning were retained in the memory, and passed
on in this way from one age to another, there being an
aversion to their arrangement in written form '. This
applies also to the Midrashim ; in regard to these
Abelson says :

' The researches of Zunz, Hoffmann, Bacher, and
others, would lead us to stretch back the origin of
Midrash to the age of the " Soferim ". These " Soferim ",
besides orally translating the Law into the vernacular,
added interpretations of their own, which, after being
orally handled by successive generations, became finally

[1] *The Immanence of God in Rabbinical Literature*, pp. 357 ff.
(1912)

written down in the earliest Midrashim, such as *Sifra, Mechilta, Bereshit Rabba,* &c. Indeed, the early origin of much Midrashic literature is seen from the fact that traces of it are to be found in many of the pre-Christian Apocalypses, as well as in the Apocrypha, the works of Josephus and Philo, and in some of the lesser known specimens of Jewish-Hellenistic literature.' [1]

But it is not sufficient to know the approximate dates of the origin and development of the material comprised in Talmud and Midrashim from which, to a large extent, we gather *data* concerning the Jewish Liturgy. We require to have some reasonable certainty that what we are told in these documents regarding liturgical matters not only goes back to pre-Christian times, but *can be regarded as reliable.* We shall, in the next chapter, when dealing with the individual elements of the Liturgy, give detailed proofs in some cases, presumptive evidence in others, that they are pre-Christian. At present we are only concerned with some general considerations to show the trustworthiness of our sources.

There are various lines of argument which go to show the reliability of the statements in these authorities. It will hardly be expected that all these should be brought forward here, for this would take us too far afield ; nor will it be expected that we should go into any great detail in those arguments which we bring. forward, for this would lead us into paths far from the main subject of these pages. It must suffice to indicate, rather than to examine and enlarge upon, some of these lines of argument.

[1] *Op. cit.,* pp. 358 ff.

I

It must strike one as noteworthy that the Old Testament contains so many genealogies. We will not give all the references to these, but they number over thirty,[1] and some of them are lengthy. In the time of Ezra and Nehemiah, and onwards, we find an increasing importance attached to genealogies, see, for example, Ezra vii. 1–6, viii. 1–14 ; Neh. vii. 6–59, xii. 1–26 ; they were, therefore, written down (Neh. vii. 5 ; Ezek. xiii. 9) ; priestly genealogies were especially important. We find that in later times also there was the same importance attached to genealogies, see the Hebrew subscription to the *Wisdom of Ben Sira* ; also 1 Macc. ii. 1 (Mattathias) ; Tob. i. 1 (Tobit) ; Bar. i. 1 (Baruch), and in the Gospels, Matt. i. 1–17 ; Lk. iii. 23–38 ; eloquent, too, is the testimony of Josephus, who gives his own genealogy, and also shows that genealogies were preserved in the public records ; he says (*Vita*, §i) : ' I will, accordingly, set down my progenitors in order . . . thus have I set down the genealogy of my family as I have found it described in the public records.' Note this last fact.

Josephus makes a special point of priestly descent, saying that his family had ' descended all along from the priests '. We have just seen that in the time of Ezra priestly genealogies had a special importance attached to them. In this connexion another quotation from Josephus is worth giving, as it shows that in his day (he lived during most of the first century A.D.)

---

[1] A convenient enumeration is given by Hirsch, *JE* v. 596 *a* f. In this the Jews were like the Arabs ; see Robertson Smith, *Kinship and Marriage in Early Arabia*, pp. 1 ff. (1903).

a similar importance was attached to priestly genealogies, and that a strict written record of them was preserved in Jerusalem ; the passage is in *Contra Ap.* i. 7 : 'For our forefathers did not only appoint the best of these priests . . . but made provision that the stock of the priests should continue unmixed and pure ; for he who is partaker of the priesthood must propagate of a wife of the same nation . . . he is to make a scrutiny, and take his wife's genealogy from the archives, and to procure many witnesses to it.' This applies both to priests living in Palestine and to those in the Dispersion ; the latter had to send to Jerusalem 'the names of their brides in writing, as well as those of their remoter ancestors, and signify who are the witnesses also'. Of all such marriages 'an exact catalogue' was kept.

The reason why we have drawn attention to this is that we may realize how important it was regarded by the Jews of post-exilic times to keep records of the genealogies of the important families, and, above all, of those of the religious leaders. This habit resulted in making it a matter of common knowledge during any given generation as to who the father, grandfather, and great-grandfather (to go no farther back) were of any prominent leader or teacher. This would be more especially the case with teachers, who were held in the greatest veneration ; many of their sayings, being uttered by men of recognized standing, would be regarded as authoritative, and would be remembered and quoted by their pupils. Among the Jews of the last three or four pre-Christian centuries religious learning as then understood was the most important thing in life ; and the teaching of the Scriptures, and especially of the Law, was pursued with intensive enthusiasm.

This was the special duty of the *Sopherim*, or ' Scribes'; and it is of particular importance to bear in mind that the earlier *Sopherim* (in the post-exilic sense [1]) were priests. The classical example of this is Ezra who is frequently referred to as priest and scribe, e. g. Ezra vii. 11, 12, 21 ; Neh. viii. 2, 3, 7 f. That genealogies of these priestly scribes were preserved appears from 1 Chron. ii. 55. In course of time, however, the priestly office became separated from that of the scribe, the former being occupied with purely sacerdotal duties, while the latter concentrated his activities on the study of the Law and taught the precepts of the Law to others.

The position which the Scribes occupied as early as the second century B.C. is brought out very clearly in *Ecclesiasticus*. Ben-Sira, while recognizing the world's need of craftsmen, regards their callings as of very minor importance compared with that of the scribe, as one who

> Meditateth in the Law of the Lord Most High ;
> He searcheth out the wisdom of all the ancients,
> And is occupied in prophecies ;
> He preserveth the discourses of men of renown,
> And entereth into subtleties of parables ;
> He seeketh out the hidden things of proverbs,
> And is conversant with the dark things of parables . . .
> Many praise his understanding,
> Never shall his name be blotted out ;
> His memorial shall not cease,
> And his name shall live unto generations of generations . . . (xxxix. 1–11).

[1] Scribes existed in pre-exilic times, but the term was then used in reference to an official in the royal household ; see 2 Sam. viii. 17, xx. 25 ; 2 Kings xii. 2, xviii. 8, xxv. 19, &c.

This passage is very important and significant, for it places before us exactly the conditions which brought the Mishnah into being : meditating in the Law, searching out the wisdom of the ancients, preserving the discourses of men of renown, the praise accorded to those thus occupied, the handing down of their name and memory, and therefore of their words and discourses. One could not have a clearer or more succinct description of what, in its essence, the Mishnah is. And the fact that this ' handing down ' of the name, memory, and discourses of teachers had been in vogue for several centuries before the Mishnah was compiled, shows that in it we have the results of an established use ; and this, it must be allowed, offers an important argument in favour of the trustworthiness of the sayings therein contained of the Rabbis or *Chakamim* (' Wise men ') as they were called ; a name which came to be synonymous with *Sopherim*, though originally this was not the case, see Jer. xviii. 18.

The argument is further strengthened when one contemplates the continuity of method and practice among the Jews in preserving genealogies, whereby names and dates can be verified. We have seen that this was done from the time of Ezra onwards ; and we find notices of the same thing in the Rabbinical writings. Thus, in the Mishnah, *Jebamoth* vii. 5, we read of Simon the son of Azzai, who lived in the first half of the second century A.D., that he ' found in Jerusalem a roll of genealogies ' (מְגִלַּת יוֹחֲסִין) ;[1] see also the Jerusalem Talmud, *Ta'anith* iv. 2, and cp. Midrash, *Ruth Rabba* to iv. 7 and iv. 15, and *Bereshith Rabba*,

---

[1] Cp. Neh. vii. 5, where almost the same phrase occurs : וָאֶמְצָא סֵפֶר הַיַּחַשׂ. On this genealogy cp. Dalman, *Die Worte Jesu*, i, pp. 3 ff. (1898).

lxxxii, where a 'chain of genealogies' is spoken of;
so too in *Shir ha-Shirim* to i. 1, where Solomon is said
to have started a 'genealogical chain'. Genealogies
are also often mentioned in the Gemara.[1] As Hirsch
says : 'Rabbinical sources show that with the dominance
of Ezra's influence and ideas importance came to be
attached to genealogies';[2] and for examples reference
may be made to Zunz's invaluable work, to which we
shall have to direct attention again, *Die Gottesdienstlichen Vorträge der Juden*, pp. 142 ff. (1892).

II

Another line of argument which tends to establish
confidence in much that we read in the Mishnah and
kindred literature would deal with the many cases in
which statements are corroborated by what is said in
other ancient documents. A few illustrations of this
may be given.

Simon ben Shetach, one of whose sayings is given
in *Aboth* i. 9, and who is often mentioned in the *Gemara*,
is said to have lived during the reigns of Alexander
Jannaeus (103–76 B.C.) and of his successor Alexandra ;
her Jewish name was Salome (76–67 B.C.) ; and he is
said to have exercised much influence over her.

Further, in the Mishnah tractate *Ta'anith* iii. 8
Simon ben Shetach is mentioned as a contemporary of
one Onias. Now, Josephus tells us that this man
Onias, one who was godly and powerful in prayer,
lived, and was murdered in the reign of Alexandra's
successor, Aristobulus II (67–63 B.C.).[3] Clearly, therefore, Josephus corroborates the Mishnah here. It is

---

[1] See Jastrow, *Talmud Dictionary*, under יחס, &c.
[2] *JE* v. 597 *a*.　　　　[3] *Antiq.* XIV. ii. 1.

only a small point; but it shows that, so far as the date of Simon ben Shetach is concerned, the Mishnah record has the support of independent historical authority.[1]

Again, Shammai and Hillel, very familiar names, as representative of schools of thought, in the Mishnah, are thus spoken of by Jerome: ' Sammai et Hellel non multo prius quam Dominus nasceretur orti sunt Judaea' (*Ad Jesai.* viii. 11 ff.).[2]

Very significant is the fact that, so far as liturgical *data* are concerned, the most important elements of the synagogue worship mentioned in the Mishnah are referred to in the New Testament. We deal with the details of this later, so that there is no need to do more here than mention the fact.

Some of the names of the most important Rabbis spoken of in the Mishnah occur elsewhere as well. Thus, Gamaliel, who is mentioned in the Mishnah, *Aboth* i. 6, was St. Paul's teacher, at whose feet he sat (Acts xxii. 3). In *Sotah* xv. 18, it is said of Gamaliel that ' when he died the honour of the Law ceased, and purity and piety became extinct'; the statement is somewhat exaggerated, but in essence it agrees closely with what St. Paul says of his having been instructed by his teacher ' according to the strict manner of the law of our fathers'. The position of honour which Gamaliel enjoyed among his people is seen from the fact that he was one of the few to whom was accorded the title of ' Rabban', a more honourable one than 'Rabbi', just as 'Rabbi' was more honourable than ' Rab'. This, together with much else which is said of Gamaliel, is borne out by Acts v. 34, where he

---

[1] Cp. Schürer, *Op. cit.*, ii. 421.
[2] Quoted by Schürer, *Op. cit.*, ii. 421.

D

is spoken of as 'a doctor of the law, had in honour of all the people'. He was the grandson of Hillel. The date of his death is given as A.D. 52.[1]

Again, Gamaliel's son, Simeon, is mentioned in *Aboth* i. 17, as having said: 'All my days have I grown up amongst the wise, and I have not found aught good for man but silence. Not the study of the Law, but its carrying out is the essential thing.' This entirely bears out Josephus' description of him as a vigorous man of action, and as one of 'great wisdom and reason, capable of restoring public affairs by his prudence'.[2] As the great-grandson of Hillel he is well described by Josephus as 'of the city of Jerusalem, and of a very celebrated family (γένους δὲ σφόδρα λαμπροῦ) of the sect of the Pharisees, reputed to excel others in the accurate knowledge of the laws of their country'.[3] Elsewhere Josephus speaks of him as 'the son of Gamaliel'.[4]

These are, then, a few examples showing that the names and sayings of teachers mentioned in the Mishnah occur also in other writings of earlier date. And this is a fact which tends to establish the reliability of the Mishnah statements.

III

In this connexion the subject of the *oral tradition* is worth a little consideration. The oral tradition was

---

[1] See the further references to Gamaliel in later Christian literature, Schürer, *Op. cit.*, ii, pp. 430 ff.

[2] A good illustration of his wisdom and reasonableness occurs in the *Tosephta*, ii. 13, to the Mishnah tractate *Sanhedrin* i. 2, where he shows the futility of making regulations for people which they cannot be expected to fulfil.

[3] *Vita*, § 38 ; see also §§ 39, 44.

[4] *Vita*, § 60 ; *Bell. Jud.* IV. iii. 9.

mainly concerned with interpretations and explanations of legal precepts contained in the Pentateuch. There were many things which were ambiguous when put to a practical test, and new conditions and altering circumstances often demanded supplementary laws which were not contained in the written law, but which, it was held, were potentially enfolded within it. The oral law thus deduced from the written law would naturally come to be regarded as equally binding with it, the more so in that the decisions were the result of thought and study applied to the written law by the authoritative religious leaders of the people. It was, on the face of it, a prime necessity that this body of traditional law should be preserved and handed down ; and since written additions to the Pentateuch were not permitted, the handing down had to be done by word of mouth. Further, it was in the nature of things that in regard to the interpretations of the written law there should be differences of opinion on many points. When such differences occurred among authoritative legalists, and unanimity could not be secured, the wisest course would be that which was actually adopted, as the later evidence proves, viz. *all* the various opinions were handed down, the point at issue being left to be decided by later authorities on the merits of each individual case that might arise.

It is characteristic of the Rabbinical literature generally that the authority of a particular teacher's name for a particular *dictum* or decision is usually indicated ; often the authority is traced back through more than one name to the original author.[1] It is

---

[1] E.g. in *Aboth* iii. 12 : 'R. Dosthai ben R. Jannai said in the name of R. Meir . . .'; in many other cases a saying is traced back through more names.

obvious that great importance was attached to the authoritative tradition of names, and great care was taken to perpetuate them correctly. Though in some cases the same *dictum* is ascribed to different teachers, it is usually possible to correct such errors by the comparison of parallel texts. It is clear, therefore, that, on the whole, the tradition is trustworthy. Indeed, where the tradition is sometimes in error (as can be demonstrated) it is in ascribing too late an authority for a particular maxim or doctrine.

When the oral law first began to come into existence it is impossible to say; nor should we expect it to be otherwise, for a thing of this kind is not noted in its beginnings; it arises too spontaneously and informally; it is only when the use has been handed down for some time that it becomes authoritative and therefore recognized. So that when it is first mentioned in literature we may rightly assume a preceding period of considerable length prior to this.

A clear indication of its existence is given by Ben-Sira, though he evidently does not approve of the methods employed; it must, however, be remembered that Ben-Sira shows himself to be somewhat antagonistic to what were to him the 'modern' Sopherim;[1] his own attitude (see the quotation on p. 22 above) appears to have been more conservative. The passage in question is xxxii (xxxv) 15–17:

He that seeketh out the Law shall gain her,
But the hypocrite shall be snared thereby;
He that feareth Yahweh discerneth judgement,
And causeth guiding lights to go forth from darkness.
The violent man shunneth reproofs,
And wresteth the Law to suit his need.

[1] See the present writer's *Ecclesiasticus* (in the Cambridge Bible), p. xxvi (1912).

Whatever else may be implied by these words, there can be no doubt that the seeking of the Law of Yahweh, which was the cultivating of 'the fear' of Him, and which caused guiding lights to the perplexed (i.e. those in 'darkness'), denoted the interpretation of the Law, upon which the oral law was founded.   See also xxxiv (xxxi) 21–31.   That Ben-Sira took a leading part in handing down the oral law may be regarded as certain on account of the mention (in li. 23) of his 'house of instruction', to which he bids the 'unlearned' come ; the phrase he uses, *Beth ha-Midrash* ('house of instruction'), is the technical one ; it was a kind of lecture hall in which recognized authorities on the Law gathered their pupils and instructed them.

While Ben-Sira represents the older school of traditionalists who later formed the party which we know by the name of the Sadducees, those teachers whom he regards as 'wresting the Law' for their own needs, and who were forming a new school of interpretation, represent the school of thought which in subsequent times came to be known as that of the Pharisees. The activities of those two schools of thought must have been greatly curtailed during the restless period of the Maccabaean struggle (175–125 B.C.) ; but they emerge after this date as two distinct and opposing parties.   Their activities during the last century B.C. must have been great, and their controversies clearly made them bitter antagonists.   Illuminating light is thrown upon the whole subject by the 'Fragments of a Zadokite Work', belonging to the last decade B.C., and written by one who was a member of the Zadokite party, which was a kind of reformed Sadduceeism. The Zadokites were as strongly opposed, if not more so, to the Pharisees as their forbears.   In this work there are various passages in which the writer inveighs against certain things which we know from later evidence to have characterized Pharisaic teaching. Thus, as Charles points out, and as seems probable, the reference in vii. 1, 'the builders of a wall who walk after law', is to the Pharisees who boasted of having made a fence round the law (see *Aboth* i. 1). In ix. 21 ff. it is said : ' But despite all these things [i. e. the punishments of the Messiah's enemies] they who builded the wall and daubed it with untempered mortar perceived not . . . that the wrath of God was kindled against all His congregation, nor that Moses said to Israel, " Not for thy righteousness nor for the uprightness of thy heart dost thou go in to inherit these nations, but because He loved thy fathers and because He would keep the oath ".' Here there is an evident allusion to the observance of legal precepts, including especially those of the oral law, which was regarded as meritorious by the Pharisees. And, once more, it is said in ix. 26 : ' But since He hated the builders of the wall His wrath was kindled.' In all probability another phrase, that of 'removing the landmark', is applied to the Pharisees. Judgement is pronounced against those who ' turn aside from the paths of righteousness, and remove the landmark which the forefathers had set in their inheritance ' (i. 11, cp. viii. 1) ; in ix. 12, 13, those who have removed the landmark are those who have ' entered into His covenant '. Against the Pharisees, to quote Charles, ' our author could bring the charge of removing " the landmark which the forefathers had set ", i. e. of introducing innovations in the ritual of the Temple and the interpretation of the Law. It is to be remembered in this connexion that although in the earlier years of Jannaeus [he reigned from 103–76 B.C.] the Pharisees were persecuted, in the later years of this king they were on friendly terms with him, whereas the Sadducean priesthood was mercilessly dealt with by him.' [1]

In this connexion the following passage from Josephus (*Antiq.* XIII. x. 6) may be quoted, especially as it offers instructive evidence on the subject of the oral tradition :

'The Pharisees have delivered to the people a great many observances by succession from their fathers, which are not written in the laws of Moses ; and for that reason it is that the Sadducees reject them, and say, that we are to esteem those observances to be obligatory which are in the written word, but are not to observe what are derived from the tradition of our forefathers. And concerning these things it is that great disputes and differences have arisen among them . . .'

Further evidence regarding the oral tradition occurs in some well-known passages in the Gospels which may be briefly referred to. Mk. vii. 3–5 : 'For the Pharisees, and all the Jews, except they wash their hands diligently, eat not, holding the tradition of the elders . . .'; vii. 9 : 'Full well do ye reject the commandment of God, that ye may keep your tradition' (=Matt. xv. 1 ff.) ; Gal. i. 14 : '. . . being more exceedingly zealous for the traditions of my fathers'; and see the references in the Sermon on the Mount to the oral tradition, Matt. vi. 1, 7, 16; cp. also Acts xviii. 15, xxiii. 29; Lk. xi. 42, 46, 52, xiv. 1–6; Gal. ii. 16; Phil. iii. 5; Eph. ii. 9.

There is thus ample evidence of the existence of the oral tradition in pre-Christian times. This remained oral until a great mass of it was compiled by Rabbi

---

[1] *Apocrypha and Pseudepigrapha of the Old Testament*, ii. 801 (1913).

Judah ha-Nasi soon after the year A. D. 200, when he reduced it to writing. What had been repeated from mouth to mouth, in some cases for at least five hundred years previously, and had thus assumed the importance and authority of a second Law, was embodied in what came to be called the ' Mishnah ', from the root *shanah* 'to repeat'. It is to this that Jerome refers when he says (*Ep*. 121) : ' I would fail to tell of the multitude of the traditions of the Pharisees, which are now called δευτερώσεις ("repetitions").'

That the date (A. D. 200) of the compilation of the Mishnah is approximately correct can be gathered from the following consideration : we have seen the importance placed upon genealogies by the Jews ; so that when we get what is, in effect, a genealogical table in the Mishnah there is presumptive evidence for regarding it as reliable, especially when it deals with some of the most revered personalities in the nation. From chapter i of the tractate *Aboth* we are able to compile this genealogy : Gamaliel, the grandson of Hillel, had a son Simeon, whose son was Gamaliel, whose son was Simeon, whose son was Judah ha-Nasi. We know that St. Paul's teacher, Gamaliel, must have lived during the first half of the first century A. D., which accords with the traditional date among the Jews ; that being so, the traditional date of the death of Gamaliel's great-great-grandson, Judah ha-Nasi (*circa* A. D. 220), is quite in accordance with probabilities.

But if the date of the compilation of the Mishnah is about A. D. 200, it means that what it records is prior to this date.[1]   True, the Mishnah has undergone

---

[1] Elbogen says that ' for the history of the Liturgy the Mishnah must be regarded as a *late* source ; even in its most ancient parts the liturgical elements are presented in an already greatly advanced stage ;

redactions since the first compiler's day; and but for one fact this might leave one often in great uncertainty as to the period to which any particular passage belonged; that fact is that in Rabbinical literature (whether Mishnah, Tosephta, Gemara, or Midrashim) in most cases the exact origin of a saying or passage is indicated by giving the name of the Rabbi who uttered it, or else by well-understood formulas; in the case of a *Tanna* ('Teacher' who lived before A.D. 200) the saying is introduced by the words: 'Our masters have handed down'; and in the case of an *Amora* ('Interpreter', who lived after A.D. 200) by the words: 'It has been said.' In general, moreover, Tannaitic matter is in neo-Hebrew, the rest in Aramaic.

But it must be remembered that those passages which belong to times after A.D. 200 often embody material of much earlier date. As Fiebig points out in this connexion:

'The materials of which the Rabbinical literature is composed were originally transmitted orally, they were thus appropriated, through the memory, by means of oral tradition. This entire literature consists, in general, not of lengthy dissertations, but of short utterances of individual men, ultimately ranged round the Old Testament and intended to be a commentary on the Old Testament. Now since the scribal activity absorbed practically the whole higher intellectual life of the Jews during the first five Christian centuries and pulsated in the 'houses of learning', it follows that the Rabbinical literature represents the deposit of Jewish intellectual activity of this epoch, taking, in the main, the form of citations.'[1]

the ground-forms and the structure of the public Liturgy are in fact determined, and, in the main, exhibit the same form as that which exists at the present day'.

[1] *Die Gleichnisreden Jesu*, p. 1 (1912).

These various considerations (and they could be greatly augmented) tend to show that reliability is to be placed in the statements of the Mishnah, &c., when used with discrimination. Our concern is solely with liturgical *data*, and the references to be utilized will all be from material belonging to the earliest *strata* contained in the Mishnah, or, when from other parts of the Rabbinical literature, from such passages as may reasonably be assumed to embody early material.

In the liturgical domain there are two factors especially which inspire confidence in the evidence of the Mishnah : first, the obvious fact that all which deals with the records of worship is naturally treated with special reverence, and is therefore the more likely to have been handed down with scrupulous exactitude. And secondly, in this domain other materials exist which, when compared with the Mishnah details, testify to its reliability ; we refer to the ancient Jewish Service books. These may, in conclusion, be briefly enumerated. There is first the tractate *Sopherim* ; as this belongs to about A. D. 600 it comes fairly soon after the close of the Talmudical period, *circa* A.D. 500. This tractate gives a connected and detailed account of the Jewish Liturgy in chaps. xvi–xxi ; what enhances its importance is that it is of Palestinian origin. Then there are various collections of liturgical prayers which have been made from time to time, and other early writings dealing specifically with the Liturgy ; these contain a mass of traditional matter regarding the content, order, and ceremonial of the services both of the Temple and of the Synagogue. The earliest extant collection of prayers is what is called the ' Hundred Benedictions ' of Natronai (*circa* A.D. 860). The first actual Jewish Prayer-Book known is that of

Amram (*circa* A.D. 875). The next in date is the *Siddur* ('Order' of prayers = the biblical עֶרֶך) of Sa'adya (A. D. 892–942); then follows the great *Machsor*[1] *Vitry*,[2] compiled by Simcha ben Samuel, of Vitry (*circa* A.D. 1100). Next is *Mishneh Tôrah* (concluding book) of Maimonides (1180) and, belonging to the same period, the *Minhag*[3] of Abraham ben Nathan ha-Jarchi: and, finally, David Abudraham's commentary on the Prayer-Book (A.D. 1340).[4]

[1] I.e. 'Order' of prayers, but one which gives more detail than a *Siddur*.

[2] A place in the extreme north-west of France.

[3] I.e. 'use'.   [4] See Elbogen for details, *Op. cit.*, pp. 6 ff.

II

THE PRE-CHRISTIAN ELEMENTS IN THE JEWISH LITURGY

We have now to indicate what parts of the Jewish Liturgy are pre-Christian; for this is an indispensable preliminary to our main task of showing in what respects early Christian forms of worship exhibit marks of Jewish influence. We shall, therefore, marshal the various elements in the Jewish Liturgy which come into consideration here, and state the reasons for regarding them as pre-Christian; while in Chapter V detailed illustrations will be offered showing their influence on early forms of Christian worship.

To decide what parts of the Jewish Liturgy are pre-Christian is sometimes a complicated matter; for its present form represents the growth of many centuries, and most of its elements have developed through the accretion of later material. Each of its component parts has to be studied individually in the light shed by various historical documents; but even so it is at times impossible to say with certainty what its original form was. At the same time the study of the whole subject has been facilitated by the labours of such scholars as Baer, Zunz, Dukes, Perles, Abrahams, and Elbogen—to mention but a few; to these and others the present writer has to express great indebtedness.

Before we come to details it may be said that, speaking generally, we are justified in stating that the earliest sources of the Mishnah show that the three ordinary daily services of the Jewish Liturgy consisted, already in pre-Christian times, of two primary elements : (i) the *Reading of Scripture*, and (ii) *Prayer*. As to the first, the Torah (the Pentateuch) was read on Mondays and Thursdays, and on feast-days. On Sabbaths and feast-days there was read, in addition to the Pentateuch lesson, a passage from the prophetical books. These were, of course, always read in Hebrew; but there followed immediately a translation in the vernacular, and an explanatory exposition.

Regarding the second, there were two parts : (*a*) the *Shema'*, and (*b*) the *Tephillah* (*Shemôneh 'Esreh*). The *Shema'*, which was recited at the morning and afternoon services, stood within a framework of liturgical pieces; at the morning and afternoon services two of these (*Yôtzer* and *'Ahabah*) preceded it, and one (*Geullah*) followed it. At the evening service the same two preceded it, but in addition to *Geullah* a second piece (*Hashkibenu*) was also said after it. This second piece took the place of the *Tephillah* which was not said at the evening service. The second part (the *Tephillah*) consisted of Praise, Petitions, and Thanksgivings.

Although this is all the information on the structure of the Liturgy given in the earliest sources of the Mishnah,[1] there were other elements belonging to the daily services which date from pre-Christian times. These will come before us as we proceed.

Our main endeavour in what follows is, firstly, to enumerate those elements of the Jewish Liturgy which, in their origin, are pre-Christian; and, secondly, to produce evidence both from early post-biblical Jewish

---

[1] Mention is made of psalms, but not in connexion with the daily services in the Synagogue worship; the passages in question deal only with their use in the Temple Liturgy.

Literature, and from other sources, to prove that they date from pre-Christian times.

The order in which the elements of the Jewish Liturgy are dealt with is not intended to be chronological, for the first beginnings of all of them are shrouded in obscurity, so that it is impossible to say which element originally preceded another. Nor is the order that of the present Jewish Liturgy, for this has gone through many stages of development, and the order of the services is very far from always having been the same. Our system is to begin with those elements which are mentioned in the earliest sources of the Mishnah, and to take the others in what we conceive to be the order of their importance.

I. The Reading of Scripture.

From very early times it has been the custom to read portions from the Pentateuch at public worship. The antiquity of the practice may be gathered from the fact that it was believed to have been enjoined by Moses himself: '. . . When all Israel is come to appear before the Lord thy God in the place which He shall choose, thou shalt read this law before all Israel in their hearing' (Deut. xxxi. 9 ff.). But more important is the account of the reading of Law contained in Ezra viii. In verses 2, 3 of this chapter it is recorded that 'Ezra the priest brought the law before the congregation, both men and women, and all that could hear with understanding, upon the first day of the seventh month. And he read therein . . . in the presence of the men and the women, and of those that could understand ; and the ears of all the people were attentive unto the book of the law' (see also verse 18). From the verses which follow the impression is gained that something very much like a form of public worship was taking place. So that Elbogen's suggestion is justified when he says that it is probable that the reading of Scripture gave the first impulse to regular assemblies for divine worship—of course in the synagogal sense, as distinct from the revived Temple worship. At any rate, there are good grounds for believing, as Elbogen shows,[1] that as a fixed, regular institution the reading of the Law at gatherings for worship can be dated not later than the middle of the third century B.C. The custom began, as Dr. Thackeray has pointed out, with

'short lessons on the Festivals and on four extraordinary sabbaths. These primitive festival lessons, we may confidently assert, were all taken from a single chapter, Lev. xxiii, containing a catalogue of feasts with instructions as to ritual. The Mishnah names lessons from this chapter for three festivals (Passover, New Year's Day, Tabernacles), and the same rule doubtless once applied to all. . . . These festival lessons from Leviticus were the first stage. The next was probably the introduction of weekly sabbath readings according to a triennial cycle. The Pentateuch was divided into some 150 sections, and was read through once in three years.'[2]

This was the system which was in use at the beginning of the Christian era; for how long previously cannot now be determined.

The lesson from the Prophets was first introduced at a somewhat later time, and, like that from the Pentateuch, it began by being read on the festivals.

---

[1] *Op. cit.*, p. 159.

[2] *The Septuagint and Jewish Worship*, pp. 43 ff. (1921).

Thackeray has some very interesting remarks on the origin of the prophetical lesson ; he infers, and his inference has much probability, that 'before the formal reception of the prophetical books into the Canon [about 200 B.C.], the custom had already grown up of chanting a canticle, or reading some edifying passage, as a sequel to the Leviticus lesson, and that this passage became the nucleus of the *Haphtarah*'.[1]

Originally the lessons were not long ; sometimes they consisted of only a few verses. As far as the lesson from the Prophets was concerned, the reader himself decided how much should be read. Any Israelite was entitled to read the lessons (*Gittin* v. 8) ; but if a priest, or a Levite, happened to be in the congregation he took precedence. When reading the Scriptures it was always customary to stand (*Yoma* vii. 1 ; *Sota* vii. 7), though, according to *Megilla* iv. 1, the reader could either stand or sit.

On the subject of Scripture reading as an element in the synagogal service see further, Lk. iv. 17–21 ; Acts xiii. 15, xv. 21 ; Josephus, *Antiq.* XVI. ii. 3, *Contra Ap.* ii. 17 ; Mishnah, *Megilla* iii. 4–6, iv. 3–6 ; among modern works, Zunz, *Op. cit.*, pp. 2 ff.; Schürer, *Op. cit.*, ii. 531 ff. ; Abrahams, *Op. cit.*, pp. lxxviii ff. ; *RWS*², pp. 380 ff. ; *SLRJ*, pp. 182, 192 ff. ; Elbogen, *Op. cit.*, pp. 155 ff. ; Thackeray, *Op. cit.*, pp. 40 ff. ; *JE* vii. 647 f. Lectionaries belong to a later time ; on these see Büchler in the *JQR* v. 420 ff. (1893), vi. 1 ff. (1894) ; Elbogen, *Op. cit.*, pp. 155 ff., 159 ff.

---

[1] *Op. cit.*, p. 45. Haphtarah is the later technical term for the prophetical lesson ; it means 'dismissal', or perhaps 'conclusion', as it came at the end of the service. The technical name for the Pentateuchal lesson was *Parashah* ('section').

II. THE EXPOSITION.

This is closely connected with the preceding ; indeed, the two form parts of the same subject. The origin of the exposition of Scripture must be sought in the time of Ezra, for in Neh. viii. 8 we read : 'And they read in the book, in the law of God, distinctly (or "with an interpretation"); and they gave the sense, so that they understood the meaning.' This explanation of Scripture is but the first step in preaching the Word. From it the Targums arose ; and these explanatory translations of the Hebrew Scriptures into the vernacular are sermons in germ. The passage just quoted was understood by the Rabbis to refer to the origin of the Targums,[1] which were spoken interpretations handed down orally for centuries before they were committed to writing.[2] 'Not only the language of the holy books, but also their contents required interpretation', says Zunz ; and this is illustrated by what is said in 2 Chron. xvii. 9 of the priests and Levites who 'taught in Judah, having the book of the law of the Lord with them ; and they went about throughout all the cities of Judah and taught among the people'.

It is thus evident that centuries before the beginning of the Christian era the custom of the public reading of passages from the Pentateuch, followed by an exposition, was in vogue ; and the same applies to the reading and exposition from the prophetical books, though in this case the custom cannot have begun, as we have seen, until approximately two centuries before the Christian era.

Details regarding the various rules to be observed

---

[1] *BT, Megilla,* 3 *a.* [2] See further *SLRJ,* pp. 43 ff.

in connexion with both the reading of Scripture and the exposition on festivals, sabbaths, and week-days are given in the Mishnah, *Megilla* iv. 1–6. Among other things it is said that no Scripture reading or exposition may not take place if less than ten men are present (iv. 3). All that is said in this tractate on the subject records current custom, which, as we have seen, had been handed down for ages.

Further evidence is gained from the New Testament. Thus, from Lk. iv. 16 ff. we are able to see that the exposition followed the Scripture reading in the ordinary way. In this instance it is Christ Himself who both reads and expounds; this was not necessarily always done; one might read and another expound, just as in the case of the Targum after the sacred text had been read. In Acts xiii. 14–16 it is apparently different: ' And after the reading of the law and the prophets the rulers of the synagogue sent unto them, saying, Brethren, if you have any word of exhortation for the people, say on. And Paul stood up, and beckoning with the hand said . . .' Here St. Paul was evidently not the reader. In passing, it may be noted that St. Paul stood up while speaking; Christ sat down (Lk. iv. 20).

That the exposition based on the reading of Scripture was a prominent element in the worship of the Synagogue long before Christian times is thus indubitable. See further Zunz, *Op. cit.*, pp. 342 ff.; Schürer, *Op. cit.*, ii. 535; *RWS*², pp. 380 ff.; *SLRJ*, pp. 43 ff.

III. The Shema'.

The nearest approach to a creed in the Jewish Liturgy was the *Shema'*. Foremost among the declarations of faith, says Abrahams, 'was the *Shema*ʿ opening with the enunciation of the unity and uniqueness of God' (Deut. vi. 4).[1]

'Now this passage,' he continues, 'like the Decalogue, was part of the daily office of the Temple (Mishnah, *Tamid* v. 1). The *purpose* of this recital is not stated in the sources, but it can hardly be that it was introduced merely as a scriptural lesson. It was not only an important text in itself, but was the most significant of the "confessional" passages of the Old Testament. For the phraseology is remarkable. Four verses of the Hebrew Bible open with the invocation: "Hear, O Israel". All four occur in Deuteronomy (v. 1, vi. 4, ix. 1, xx. 3). Now, in all but the one before us (vi. 4) the invocation is followed up by the *second* person; only here is the *first* person used ("the Lord *our* God"). The older Midrashim perceived this verbal difference. "The Lord our God the Lord is one",— the Lord who in the first instance is our (Israel's) God, is to be the One God also to the nations (quoting Zech. xiv. 9; *Sifre* on Deut. vi. 4). This conception enormously added to the importance of the text as a testimony to God, and there seems no reason to doubt that the exegesis was ancient. The whole idea of witnessing to God was, moreover, of this twofold nature; it was a personal acknowledgement by Israel, it was a universal proclamation to the world. . . . In the Synagogue liturgy the recital of the *Shema*ʿ is followed by the clearest declaration of faith known to

---

[1] It was not until the twelfth century that a creed in the stricter sense was compiled. This was what is called the 'Thirteen Principles of the Faith', founded on the teaching of Maimonides in his commentary on the Mishnah, and therefore known as the 'Creed of Maimonides'. Each of the principles begins with, 'I believe with perfect faith'. It is now incorporated in the Liturgy in two forms, one in prose and the other in poetry; the latter is known as *Yigdal*, from the opening word, '*Magnified* be the living God'. On the subject generally see Schechter, *Studies in Judaism*, pp. 197 ff. (1896).

the Hebrew prayer-book. " Yea, *it is true*—this thy
word. . . . *It is true* that the God of the Universe is
our King." This passage, based (on the authority of
Rab) on Ps. xcii. 3, is the nearest to a Creed that the
Synagogue liturgy ever attained before the late Middle
Ages. In essence the passage is old, belonging,
according to the best authorities, to the period of the
Hasmonean revival.' [1]

The passage he quotes is from *Geullah*, with which
we deal below. We have cited this somewhat lengthy
extract because in it Dr. Abrahams brings out so
admirably the truth of the *Shema'* being a confession
of faith. It is a subject to which we shall return in a
later chapter.[2]

While originally, in its liturgical use, the *Shema'*
consisted only of Deut. vi. 4 (' Hear, O Israel; the
Lord our God is One Lord '), its present full form,
consisting of Deut. vi. 4–9, xi. 13–21; Num. xv. 37–41,
was an integral part of the Temple Liturgy (*Tamid*
v. 1).

That it was a pre-Christian element in the Jewish
Liturgy the following considerations will show :

(*a*) The discussions of the ' schools ' of Hillel and
Shammai on various points connected with the recita-
tion of the *Shema'* (see the Mishnah, *Berakhôth* i. 5;
Tosephta, Berakhôth i. 4) prove that it was a pre-
Christian element in the Liturgy. Other references in the
Mishnah point to the same fact. Thus from *Tamid* i. 1
we learn that the *Shema'* not only belonged to the
Temple Liturgy, but that it was taken over from there
by the Synagogue. Again, in *Abôth* ii. 17 it is said :
' Be careful in reading the *Shema'* and in (offering)

[1] *Studies in Pharisaism and the Gospels*; Second Series, pp. 18 ff.
(1924).
[2] See pp. 121 ff.

prayer'; this was a saying of Rabbi Simeon, a pupil of Jochanan ben Zakkai (*circa* A.D. 70). In *Berakhôth* i. 4 the precise time at the morning and evening recitation of the *Shema'* is discussed (see also iii. 3) ; and in i. 5 directions are given as to the posture to be assumed while reciting it. Other passages in which the *Shema'* is dealt with are : *Megilla* iv. 3–6; *Ta'anith* ii. 1, iv. 3 ; *Sota* v. 4, vii. 1 ; *Pesachim* iv. 8 ; *Shekalim* viii. 8 ; *Tamid* iv. 1–3, vii, and elsewhere. When it is remembered that the Mishnah, which, as we have seen, was compiled in its official written form soon after A.D. 200, embodies traditions which in many cases have been handed down for centuries previously, it will be realized that we are dealing with ancient material.

(*b*) A further indication of the antiquity of the *Shema'* is to be seen in the fact that the three sections of which it is composed (see above) came to be known respectively by their initial words as their titles ; these titles are referred to in the Mishnah, *Berakhôth* ii. 1, 2. Every liturgical piece has its name in the Liturgy ; but for it to be known by its name in this way shows clearly that it must have been incorporated for some considerable time previously.

(*c*) The *Shema'* is referred to by Christ in Mk. xii. 29 ; that it is here thought of not only as a biblical quotation, but also as a liturgical element, is suggested by the words in the context : 'Of a truth, Master, Thou hast well said, and to love ... is much more than whole burnt offerings and sacrifices.'

(*d*) The command to recite the *Shema'* twice daily is assumed by Josephus to have been given by Moses. In purporting to quote his words Josephus says : ' Let every one commemorate before God the benefits which He bestowed on them at their deliverance out of the land of Egypt, and this twice every day; both when the day begins, and when the hour of sleep comes on' (*Antiq.* IV. viii. 13). That Josephus is here referring to the recitation of the *Shema'* is certain, not only on account of his mention of the deliverance from the land of Egypt, which occurs in the third section of the *Shema'*, but also because its recitation morning and evening rests upon the interpretation of Deut. vi. 7, 'when thou liest down, and when thou risest up'.[1] And further, Josephus, in this passage, goes on to speak of the *Mezúzah*[2] and the *Tephillin*,[2] which are referred to, according to the traditional belief, in Deut. vi. 8, 9.

IV. The Shema' Benedictions.

To emphasize the veneration in which the *Shema'* was held it was, in early days, placed, as it were, within a framework of Benedictions; two preceded it and one (at the evening service two) followed it; they still form part of the Liturgy. These three liturgical pieces are known respectively, from the most important of their opening words, as: *Yôtzer* ('Creator'), *'Ahabah* ('Love'), and *Emeth we-Yatzib* ('True and constant'); this last is better known as *Geullah* ('Redemption') on account of its concluding words: 'Who hast redeemed Israel.'

All three are referred to in the Mishnah (*Berakhôth* i. 4, cp. ii. 2, iii. 3, 4); *'Ahabah* and *Geullah* are quoted in *Tamid* v. 1, and in the Gemara, *Berakhôth* 11 *b*; the latter is mentioned by name in the Tosephta, *Ber.* i. 2, and in the Mishnah, *Ber.* ii. 2. The reference to

---

[1] Cp. Mishnah, *Berakhôth* i. 3.

[2] On these see *RWS*[2], pp. 454 ff., 447 ff.

a liturgical piece by its title shows how well known it was at the time ; and this suggests that it had formed part of the Liturgy long previously. There can be little doubt that, in their original forms, *'Ahabah* and *Geullah*, and probably *Yôtzer* too, were used in the Temple Liturgy.

A few words on each of these three important liturgical pieces will not be out of place.

(*a*). *Yôtzer*. This Benediction offers a good illustration of the way in which liturgical pieces have, in the course of ages, been lengthened from time to time by the addition of new matter. *Yôtzer* is a particularly good example because its unnecessary redundancy gives one the impression at once that its present form is not the original one. There is a heaping-up of phrases and expressions which, according to all ancient evidence, was not characteristic of liturgical pieces in the early stages of their existence. Particularly noticeable in *Yôtzer* is the fact that it contains two alphabetical acrostics, one complete and the other incomplete ; but, as Elbogen points out, these had not yet been incorporated in the Geonic period,[1] and cannot therefore have formed part of the Benediction until about the beginning of the seventh century A. D. at the earliest. But although *Yôtzer* as we now have it has preserved the additions of more than one pietist, it dates back, as we have seen, in its original form to an early period. What the original form consisted of cannot be stated with certainty ; but, after the elimination of some demonstrably later portions, there is a high probability that at the beginning of the Christian era, if not earlier,

---

[1] *Op. cit.*, p. 18. On the Geonic period (the latter part of the sixth century to the first half of the eleventh) see *SLRJ*, pp. 25 ff., 210 ff.

its form was that for which Zunz[1] contends, and of which the following is a translation :

> Blessed art Thou, O Lord our God, King of the Universe, who formest light and createst darkness; who makest peace and createst all things; who givest light in mercy to the earth and to those who live thereon, and in goodness renewest every day continually the work of creation.[2] Be Thou blessed, O Lord our God, for the excellency of the work of Thy hands, and for the bright luminaries which Thou hast made ; let them glorify Thee. Selah. Blessed art Thou, O Lord, who formest the luminaries.

Elbogen thinks that the words 'Be Thou blessed . . .' to 'Selah' do not belong to the Benediction in its earliest form.[3]   In any case, the presence of 'Selah' points to a high antiquity.

(b) *'Ahabah.* This Benediction is much shorter than the preceding, having come down to us with but few additions.   In *Yôtzer* God is glorified as the giver of material light, in *'Ahabah* prayer is offered for spiritual light.   Abrahams truly says that this prayer is 'one of the most beautiful in the liturgies of the world '.[4]

There is not much difference of opinion among Jewish liturgical experts as to what constitutes the earliest portions of the *'Ahabah.* Following Zunz the appended translation represents approximately its original form :

> With great love hast Thou loved us, O Lord our God ; with great and overflowing pity hast Thou pitied us. O our Father, our King, for our fathers' sake, who trusted in Thee, and whom Thou didst teach the statutes of life, be gracious unto us too, and teach us. Enlighten our eyes in Thy Law,

---

[1] *Op. cit.,* pp. 382 ff.
[2] Lit. 'the work of in the beginning' (*Bereshith*).
[3] *Op. cit.,* p. 18.   [4] *Annotated Prayer-Book,* p. xlix.

and let our hearts cleave unto Thy commandments, and unite our hearts to love and fear Thy Name, that we may never be put to confusion. For a God that worketh salvation art Thou; and us hast Thou chosen from every people and tongue, and hast brought us near unto Thy great Name [Selah] in faithfulness, to give thanks unto Thee, and to proclaim Thy unity, in love. Blessed art Thou, O Lord, who choosest Thy people Israel in love.

(*c*) *Geullah.* The text of this long Benediction was originally very much shorter, though 'most of the additions must have been introduced early into the primitive form. The similarity of this part of the liturgy to the style and beauty of the biblical Hebrew is a strong confirmation of its antiquity.'[1] The writer of 4 Esdras seems to have had this Benediction in mind in viii. 22 : '. . . Whose word is *sure* (or "true"), and behest *constant* ;'[2] these two words correspond precisely to the Hebrew *Emeth*, and the Aramaic *Yatzib*, with which *Geullah* begins ; in fact, as already pointed out, its ancient title was *Emeth we-Yatzib* ; it is referred to in the Mishnah, *Tamid* v. 1, under this title. They are epithets applied in the Benediction to the 'word', i.e. the *Shema*' ; 'True and constant . . . is Thy word unto us for ever and ever.'

According to Zunz, *Geullah* consisted originally of only forty-five words; but some of the additions are of an early date. In the following translation we have included not only what Zunz believes to have been the earliest additions, but also the later ones, as there is every reason for regarding them as, at any rate, pre-Christian.

[1] Abrahams, *Op. cit.*, p. lv.

[2] Box, *The Ezra-Apocalypse*, p. 179 (1912); the main portion of this apocalypse (iii–xiv) was finally redacted early in the second century A. D.

True and constant, established and enduring, right and faithful, beloved and precious, desired and pleasant, awe-inspiring and mighty, well-ordered and acceptable, good and lovely, is this word unto us for ever and ever. True it is that the God of the universe is our King, the Rock of Jacob, the shield of our salvation. To generation and generation He endureth, and His Name endureth. And His throne is established, and His Kingdom and His faithfulness endure for ever. And His words are living and enduring, faithful and desirable for ever and unto the ages of ages, for our fathers and for us, for our children and for our generations, and for the generations of the seed of Israel Thy servants.

True it is that Thou art He who art the Lord our God, and the God of our fathers; our King, and the King of our fathers; our Redeemer, and the Redeemer of our fathers; our Maker, the Rock of our salvation; our Liberator and our Deliverer from everlasting; that is Thy Name; there is no God beside Thee.

The long passage which now follows is regarded by some scholars as a later addition; but its main content, the memorial of the deliverance from Egypt, and the fact that, as we shall show, it forms the basis of an early Christian liturgical prayer, point indubitably to its being of pre-Christian date. As we shall have occasion to quote it later (see p. 139) we shall omit it here. The text then continues:

With a new song did the redeemed praise Thy Name on the sea-shore; with one accord did they give thanks and acknowledged Thy Kingship, and said, 'The Lord shall reign for ever and ever.'

O Rock of Israel, arise to the help of Israel, and deliver, according to Thy promise, Judah and Israel. Our Redeemer, the Lord of Hosts is His Name, the Holy One of Israel. Blessed art Thou, O Lord, who hast redeemed Israel.

(*d*) *Hashkibenu* ('Cause us to lie down'). This Benediction is added at the evening service; its antiquity is not so sure as that of the three already mentioned, though a second Benediction said after the evening *Shema'* is spoken of in the Mishnah and Gemara which evidently refers to this. It is a beautiful evening prayer and must, in substance, go back to a considerable antiquity; it is, therefore, worth quoting :

> Cause us to lie down, O Lord our God, in peace ; and cause us to rise, O our King, to life. And spread over us the tabernacle of Thy peace ; and guide us by Thy good counsel. Deliver us for Thy Name's sake, and be a shield about us. Keep far from us every enemy,—pestilence and sword, hunger, and grief; drive away the evil one [*lit.* Satan] from before us and behind us. Shelter us under the shadow of Thy wings, for Thou, O God, art our Guardian and Deliverer ; for Thou, O God, art a gracious and merciful King. Guard our going out and coming in that it may be for life and peace from henceforth and for ever. Blessed art Thou, O Lord, that guardest Thy people Israel for ever.

These, then, are the *Shema'* Benedictions, and they constitute some of the gems of the Jewish Liturgy. That they exercised an influence on the early forms of Christian worship we hope to show in a later chapter.

V. Prayer.

As already pointed out, the *Shema'* with its Benedictions was regarded as the first part of the second primary element in the pre-Christian Liturgy of the Jewish Church. The other part of this second primary element was Prayer.

(*a*) The Synagogal Prayers. Regarding Prayer in general in the Synagogue it should be pointed out that although fixed forms of prayer belonged to an early period, certainly before the Christian era, yet originally the prayers were variable in form, if not in content. But daily repetition naturally tended in course of time to a fixed form of words in the prayers, though alongside of these various circumstances would arise which would call for other prayers of variable character. In any case, however, prayers were not written down until a comparatively late period, the fourth or fifth century A.D. An old Jewish sage used to say that 'he who writes down prayers sins as though he burned the Torah', the idea being that the sacred script might fall into profane hands.[1]

The characteristic notes of the Synagogue prayers are Praise and Thanksgiving to God for mercies vouchsafed, the former element being emphasized by the doxology which concludes every prayer; actual petitions, though frequent, take a subordinate position. Hence the name *Berakhah* (' Benediction ') usually applied to the prayers. The subjects of Praise and Thanksgiving are the power and might of God in His work of creation, and His guardianship of His people as seen in the course of their history; pre-eminent in the latter is the deliverance from Egypt, which finds frequent expression, and is regarded as an earnest of deliverance from evil in general.

A further element which comes to the fore in the prayers, though less prominently, is the sense of sin expressed by confession, coupled with a prayer for forgiveness. This developed as the direct outcome of the Exile and is perhaps most pointedly illustrated by the great prayer in Neh. ix. The liturgical character

---

[1] Cp. the words of Rabbi Simeon (early 1st cent. A.D.) in *Aboth* ii. 17 : 'When thou prayest make not thy prayer a mechanical formality' (*Qeba'* contains the idea of something fixed); see also *Ber.* iv. 4.

of this prayer is very marked ; it opens with praise and thanksgiving for the work of creation, for guidance, for deliverance from the Egyptian bondage, and for the giving of the Law ; the long historical retrospect is, in reality, an expression of thanksgiving. Then follows, in the concluding portion, the confession of sin, verses 32 ff. :

'Now, therefore, our God, the great, the mighty, and the terrible God, who keepest covenant and mercy. . . . Howbeit thou art just in all that is come upon us ; for thou hast dealt truly, but we have done wickedly ; neither have our kings, our princes, our priests, nor our fathers, kept thy Law, nor hearkened unto thy commandments and thy testimonies, wherewith thou didst testify against them. For they have not served thee in their kingdom, and in thy great goodness that thou gavest them, and in the large and fat land which thou gavest before them, neither turned they from their wicked works . . .' [1]

Very noticeable here is the *corporate sense* expressed in the confession of sin ; it is characteristic also of the later prayers of the Synagogue, and may be regarded, though in a restricted sense, as a Catholic sentiment in Judaism.

One other element must be noted in this brief bird's-eye view of the Jewish prayers in general, viz. intercession for others. In a prayer of the Synagogue, which will be fully dealt with below, there is a short intercession for the righteous within the community of Israel (*Shemôneh 'Esreh*, Ben. xiii) ; but there is reason to believe that intercessions were offered on behalf of those outside the community as well. In the decree of

---

[1] A good illustration of the elements referred to will be found in the liturgical prayers in 2 Macc. i. 24 ff., where, however, the confession of sin does not appear, and 3 Macc. ii. 1 ff., which is especially striking ; it belongs to about 100 B. C.

Darius, Ezra ix, the king requests that the people
should 'pray for the life of the king, and of his sons'
(verse 10); that the request was fulfilled may be
gathered from the very fact of its appearing in the
Scriptural record. A more direct instance is given by
Josephus (*Antiq.* XII. ii. 6); Eleazar, the high-priest,
in writing to the King of Egypt, Ptolemy, says '. . . We
immediately, therefore, offered sacrifices for thee and
thy sister, with thy children and friends; and the
multitude made prayers, that thy affairs may be to thy
mind, and that thy kingdom may be preserved in
peace . . .' In the Mishnah, *Aboth* iii. 2, it is said:
'Pray for the peace of the kingdom'; this has always
been understood as including the king.

Finally, there is the doxology which forms an indispensable conclusion to prayer.

(*b*) THE SHEMÔNEH 'ESREH. To come now to some
illustrations from the Jewish Liturgy itself. This
element of prayer, centred in what is known as the
Tephillah ('Prayer'), because it is the Prayer *par
excellence* of the Synagogue. It is also called the
Amidah ('Standing') because during its recital the
congregation stands. It is further known as the *Shemôneh 'Esreh* ('Eighteen', i. e. Benedictions, of which
it is composed), and is mentioned by this name in the
Mishnah, *Ber.* iv. 3, where it is said that 'Rabban
Gamaliel used to say, A man prays the Eighteen every
day' (at each of the three daily services (*Ber.* iv. 1)).
The Gamaliel here referred to is the second of the
name who lived at the end of the first century A.D.,
and during the first half of the second. The prayer
now contains nineteen Benedictions (see below), but
still bears its ancient name.

As to the date of this prayer, the contents of its

various Benedictions raise a number of problems and difficulties [1] which show that they must belong to different periods. For our present purpose, however, these difficulties need not trouble us, because, with two exceptions, the evidence points to all the Benedictions of the prayer as belonging substantially to pre-Christian times. The exceptions are the twelfth, which was added by Gamaliel II about A.D. 100,[2] and the fifteenth, which belongs to a period a century or so later.[3]

That in its original form the *Shemôneh 'Esreh* was much shorter than as we now have it is clear from a comparison of the two extant recensions, the Palestinian and Babylonian.[4] Indeed, there is reason to believe that originally it consisted of only six benedictions.

One of the most interesting indications of the early date of this liturgical piece is the parallelism in thought and expression between it and the psalm in the *Wisdom of Ben-Sira* which occurs after li. 12 in the Hebrew form. This book belongs to about 175 B.C.; and even if the psalm, as some maintain, is of later date than the rest of the book, it is, in any case, pre-Christian; and this is the main thing about it which at present concerns us. That the *Shemôneh 'Esreh* was known to the writer of this psalm may be seen by the following comparison : [5]

Ben-Sira.	*Shemôneh 'Esreh.*
Verse.	*Benediction.*
2. Give thanks unto the God of praises.	3. Holy ones praise Thee every day.

---

[1] These are dealt with by Elbogen, *Op. cit.*, pp. 27 ff.

[2] *BT, Ber.* 28 *b* (Elbogen, *Op. cit.*, p. 36).

[3] Elbogen, *Op. cit.*, pp. 39 ff.

[4] They are given by Dalman, *Die Worte Jesu*, pp. 301 ff. (1898).

[5] The identical words and phrases in the Hebrew of each are given in italics.

Verse.	Benediction.
5. Give thanks unto the *Redeemer* of *Israel*.	7. Blessed art Thou, O Lord, *the Redeemer of Israel*.
6. Give thanks unto Him *that gathereth the outcasts of Israel*.	10. Blessed art Thou, O Lord, *that gatherest the outcasts of* Thy people *Israel*.
7. Give thanks unto Him *that buildeth His City* and His Sanctuary.	14. Do thou dwell in the midst of Jerusalem *Thy City* . . . And *build* it an everlasting building speedily in our days. Blessed art Thou, O Lord, *that buildest* Jerusalem.
8. Give thanks unto Him *that causeth a horn to flourish for* the house of *David*.	15. *Do Thou cause to flourish* the branch of *David* speedily, and do Thou exalt his *horn* by Thy salvation.
10. Give thanks unto *the Shield of Abraham*.	1. Blessed art Thou, O Lord, *the Shield of Abraham*.
11. Give thanks unto the *Rock* of Isaac.	18. We give thanks unto Thee, for Thou art the Lord our God and the God of our fathers for ever and ever ; Thou art the *Rock* of our lives . . .
12. Give thanks unto the *Mighty One of Jacob*.	1. Blessed art Thou, O Lord our God and God of our fathers, the God of Abraham, the God of Isaac, and *the God of Jacob*, the great, *mighty*, and revered God . . .

Verse.	Benediction.
13. Give thanks unto Him *that hath chosen Zion*.[1]	17. May our eyes behold Thy return to *Zion* in mercy. Blessed art Thou, O Lord, *that restorest Thy Shekhinah to Zion*.[1]
14. Give thanks unto the *King* of the Kings of Kings.	11. *Reign Thou* over us, O Lord, Thou alone, in loving - kindness and mercy . . . Blessed art Thou, O Lord, *King*, that loveth righteousness and judgement.

The title 'King' applied to God occurs four times in the *Shemôneh 'Esreh* in addition to its mention in the eleventh Benediction.

Identical expressions grouped together in this way in the *Shemôneh 'Esreh* and in this psalm, respectively, cannot be fortuitous. It must be remembered that the psalm is quite short; and though the order in which these words and phrases occur differs in the two pieces, yet when they are found, respectively, within a restricted compass in this way the conviction is forced upon one that there is a fundamental connexion between the two. There is no reason to suppose that the order of the Benedictions of the *Shemôneh 'Esreh* was always the same in the earlier stages of its history; indeed, the fact that prayers were not written down until a comparatively late period would account very naturally for some diversity here. The writer of the psalm had obviously no other intention than to bring into his composition some of the key-notes of the great

---

[1] The presence of the *Shekhinah* in Zion means that God has chosen Zion.

liturgical prayer, which shows that he was very familiar with it. The similarity between verse 8 of the psalm and the fifteenth Benediction, which was not added until the third century A.D. (see further on this below), need not create surprise, for the expression in question ('making to flourish the horn of David') is derived from Ps. cxxxii. 17, which is doubtless the source in each case. Apart from this fifteenth Benediction it will be noticed that in six cases the parallels are found in the earlier Benedictions, in three cases in the later ones, viz. 10, 11, 14. In regard to these last three, if they are as late as some scholars suppose, the parallelism between them and the psalm would be due to the identity of their Old Testament source; but we doubt whether a post-Christian date for them is justified; see further below, pp. 65 f.

Hirsch suggests that Ecclus. xxxvi. 1–17 (= xxxiii. 1–13ᵃ, xxxvi. 16ᵇ–22) has 'the appearance of being an epitome of the *Tephillah* known in the days of Ben-Sira'.[1] It is true there are some parallels to be found between the two, and it is possible that Hirsch may be right; but it appears to the present writer that the differences are more pronounced than the similarities; the latter may well have been drawn from sources common to both, viz. passages from the Old Testament.

At any rate, upon the whole, there can be no doubt that we are justified in basing a strong argument for the early date of the *Shemôneh 'Esreh* upon the parallels which exist between it and the psalm.

The *Shemôneh 'Esreh*, which was recited three times daily (Mishnah, *Ber.* iv. 1), consists of three groups of Benedictions, thus: (1) the first three, (2) the last three, (3) the intervening ones. The first group

[1] In *JE* xi. 280 *b*.

contains ascriptions of praise, the last consists of thanksgivings, while the middle one is composed of petitions. The Benedictions of the first and third groups are invariable, and they are said daily throughout the year;[1] those of the second group are used only on ordinary week-days, whereas on Sabbaths and festivals and on the Day of Atonement they give place to special petitions proper to the day or season. So that the first and third group form a fixed framework between which are placed the variable Benedictions of the intermediate group.

The following version of the *Shemôneh 'Esreh* is translated from the Babylonian recension published by Dalman.[2] This is the longer form, and therefore includes the later additions, and probably approximates more closely to that with which the first Jewish Christians were familiar. Dalman believes that this recension was originally Palestinian, but that Babylon was the centre from which it spread later and became the universally accepted form. There is every reason to believe that originally the *Shemôneh 'Esreh* was composed on the pattern of early Hebrew poetry,[3] i. e. each section consisted of two lines in rhythmic measure,[4] after which came the Benediction.

For convenience' sake we give the sections in their chronological order, following Zunz in the main, viz. 1–3, 17–19; 4–9, 16; 10, 11, 13; 12, 15.

The words in square brackets are those portions which, according to Dalman, did not form part of the original Benedictions; this does not imply that the

---

[1] Mishnah, *Ta'anith* ii. 2.   [2] *Die Worte Jesu*, pp. 301–4 (1898).
[3] Abrahams, *Op. cit.*, p. lvii.
[4] This is, in the main, the form in the Palestinian recension.

words in square brackets are not, substantially, pre-Christian.

BENEDICTION i.

Blessed art Thou, O Lord our God, and the God of our fathers,

The God of Abraham, the God of Isaac, and the God of Jacob.

[God the Great One, the Mighty One, and the Revered One],

God Most High who [dost grant loving (lit. 'good') mercies and] dost possess all things;

[Who dost remember the pious deeds of the fathers, and showest compassion upon their children, and wilt bring a redeemer to their children's children for His Name's sake, in love; Merciful King, Saviour, Helper, and Shield].

Blessed art Thou, O Lord, the Shield of Abraham.

BENEDICTION ii.

Thou art mighty for ever, O Lord,

[O Thou that quickenest the dead, Thou art mighty to save],

That causest the wind to blow, and the rain to descend;

Thou sustainest the living [with mercy], Thou quickenest the dead.

[With great mercies Thou dost heal the sick, dost help the weak, dost support the fallen, dost loose the bound, and dost keep faith with them that sleep in the dust. And who is like unto Thee, Master of mighty acts? And who resembleth Thee, that killest and makest alive, and causest salvation to spring forth, that art faithful in quickening the dead?]

Blessed art Thou, O Lord, that quickenest the dead.

BENEDICTION iii.

Thou art holy, and holy is Thy Name (Selah).

And holy ones praise Thee every day.

Blessed art Thou, O Lord, the Holy God.[1]

---

[1] After this Benediction follows the *Kedûshah*, which is dealt with below, pp. 67 f.

BENEDICTION xvii.

Accept, O Lord our God, Thy people Israel [and their prayer],

And restore the service to the oracle (*debir*) of Thy House.

[And the fire-offerings of Israel and their prayer and their service do Thou speedily accept in love with favour ; and may the service of Thy people Israel be ever acceptable],

And may our eyes behold Thy return to Zion [in mercy, as of yore].

Blessed art Thou, O Lord, that restorest [speedily] Thy Shekhinah unto Zion.

BENEDICTION xviii.

We give thanks unto Thee [for Thou art He], O Lord our God, and the God of our fathers ;

[The Rock of our lives, and the Shield of our salvation art Thou from generation to generation. We give thanks unto Thee, and declare Thy praise],

For our lives which are committed into Thy hand, and for our souls which are in Thy care ;

For Thy miracles and for Thy wonders, and for Thy benefits at all times ;

[At evening and morning and midday].

[Thou art good, for Thy loving-kindnesses fail not ; Thou art merciful, for Thy mercies cease not.]

[For all the living praise Thy great Name ; for Thou art good, Thou Good God.]

Blessed art Thou, O Lord ; good [and beautiful] it is to praise Thee [and Thy Name continually].

BENEDICTION xix.

Give [goodly] peace and blessing [grace and mercy and loving-kindnesses] unto us, even unto Israel, Thy people.

Bless us altogether, O Lord our God, [in the light of Thy countenance ; for in the light of Thy countenance Thou hast given us, O Lord our God, the Law and life, love and mercy, righteousness and peace, blessing and loving-

kindnesses], yea, it is good in Thine eyes to bless Thy
people Israel [with abundance of strength and peace].
Blessed art Thou, O Lord, that blessest [Thy people Israel]
with peace. Amen.

These six Benedictions are all mentioned by name
in the Mishnah, *Rôsh Hashanah* iv. 5 ; they are there
referred to under the following names, respectively :
Abôth ('Fathers'), *Geburôth* ('Mighty acts'), *Kedushath ha-Shem* ('Sanctification of the Name'),[1] *Abodah*
('Service'), *Hoda'ah* ('Thanksgiving'), and *Birkath
ha-Kohanim* ('Blessing of the priests'). As will at
once be seen, these titles express the subject of each
respective Benediction. That these six Benedictions
were known by these titles clearly implies a long previous
history. In the seventeenth Benediction the words
'And restore the service to the oracle of Thy House'
imply that the Temple was destroyed, and they must,
therefore, belong to a later period ; the same applies
to the last two lines of this Benediction ; the last line
may well have run originally : 'Blessed art Thou,
O Lord, who hast chosen Zion'; the parallel passage
in Ben-Sira ends with : 'that hath chosen Zion'; the
Palestinian recension, however, has : 'Blessed art
Thou, O Lord ; Thee do we serve in fear.'

BENEDICTION iv.

Thou dost favourably grant knowledge unto men,
And dost teach discernment unto men ;
Grant us from Thee knowledge and understanding and dis-
cernment.
Blessed art Thou who dost graciously grant knowledge.

[1] After this, a benediction is mentioned in the Mishnah passage
referred to which is called *Kedushath ha-Yom* ('Sanctification of the
Day'), because it is a festival service that is described, and this
Benediction is used on all festivals.

BENEDICTION v.

Cause us to return, our Father, unto Thy Law;
And draw us near, our King, unto Thy service;
And bring us back in perfect repentance to Thy presence.
Blessed art Thou, O Lord, that delightest in repentance.

BENEDICTION vi.

Forgive us, our Father, for we have sinned ;
Pardon us, our King, for we have transgressed.
For Thou art the God of goodness, Thou dost forgive.
Blessed art Thou, O Lord, [Who art gracious,] Who dost
abundantly forgive.

BENEDICTION vii.

Look upon our affliction, and plead our cause, and haste to
redeem us ;
For Thou art God, [King,] Mighty Redeemer.
Blessed art Thou, O Lord, the Redeemer of Israel.

BENEDICTION viii.

Heal us, O Lord our God, and we shall be healed ;
[Save us, and we shall be saved] ;
Vouchsafe [perfect] healing to all our wounds,
For Thou, O God, art a merciful Healer.
Blessed art Thou, O Lord, that healest [the sicknesses of His
people] Israel.

BENEDICTION ix.

Bless us, O Lord our God, in all the work of our hands,
And bless our years [and give dew and rain upon the face of
the earth], and satisfy the world and its fulness with Thy
goodness.
[And give plenty upon the face of the earth through the
richness of the gifts of Thy hands ; and preserve and
prosper, O Lord our God, this year with every kind of
produce, (keeping) from it every kind of destruction and
want ; and grant to it issue and hope and plenty and
peace and blessing, as in other good years.]
Blessed art Thou, O Lord, that blessest the years.

BENEDICTION xvi.

Hear our voice, O Lord our God, [spare us] and have mercy
upon us,
And accept our prayer in mercy [and favour],
[From Thy presence, O our King, turn us not away empty]
For Thou hearest the prayer of every mouth.
Blessed art Thou that hearkenest unto prayer.

The fourth Benediction is called *Chônen ha-da'ath*
('He that graciously granteth knowledge') in the
Mishnah, *Ber.* v. 2. Zunz regards the seventh as belonging to a later date than the rest in this group,
assigning it to the beginning of the Maccabaean
struggle, in the time of Antiochus Epiphanes (he
reigned 175–164 B.C.), or at the beginning of Roman
suzerainty (Pompey, 63 B. C.). Elbogen places it earlier
and thinks that it was taken from the special Liturgy for
fast-days, in which case its position after the prayers for
repentance (fifth Benediction) and forgiveness (sixth) is
appropriate; the eighth also follows in logical sequence.
The ninth Benediction clearly presupposes an agricul-
tural people living in peace; it must, therefore, be
pre-Maccabaean, and presumably belongs to the period
of the Syrian suzerainty. It is true that in 1 Macc. x.
29, 30 tribute is mentioned as being exacted on the
produce of the soil; but that would not prevent the
people from praying for the divine blessing on their
labours. This Benediction is known under the title
of *Birkath ha-shanim* ('The Blessing of the years') in
Ber. v. 2.

BENEDICTION x.

Sound the great horn for our freedom,
And lift up the ensign to gather all our exiles from the four
corners of the earth to our own land.
Blessed art Thou, O Lord, that gatherest [the outcasts of Thy
people] Israel.

BENEDICTION xi.

Restore our judges as in former times, and our counsellors as
in the beginning,
[And put away from us grief and sighing], And do Thou
alone reign over us [in mercy, in righteousness, and in
judgement].
Blessed art Thou, O Lord [and King], that lovest [righteous-
ness and] judgement.

BENEDICTION xiii.

Upon the righteous [and upon the pious, upon the elders of
Thy people the house of Israel, upon the remnant of their
scribes], and upon the proselytes of righteousness, Let
Thy mercies be stirred, O Lord our God ;
And grant a good reward unto all that trust in Thy Name [in
truth ; and set out our portion with them for ever ; let us
not be ashamed, for in Thy Name have we trusted, and we
have relied upon Thy salvation].
Blessed art Thou, O Lord [the Stay and] the trust of the
righteous.

BENEDICTION xiv.

Do Thou dwell in the midst of Jerusalem, Thy City [according
as Thou hast said],
And build it an everlasting building speedily in our days,
Blessed art Thou, O Lord, that buildest Jerusalem.

It is difficult to assign a date for these four 'national'
Benedictions; the opinions of scholars differ considerably, though on one point there is a good deal of
agreement, viz. that they are pre-Christian. Hirsch's
contention, however, appears to us eminently reasonable
when he says: 'The Maccabaean period seems to furnish
adequate background for the national petitions, though
the experiences of the Roman war and the subsequent
disasters may have heightened the colouring in many

details.'[1] He includes the fifteenth Benediction here, an opinion which, for reasons to be given presently, we cannot share. In their *present form* they belong probably to the second half of the last pre-Christian century.

An important point about these four Benedictions is their *Messianic character*. The tenth is evidently based on Isa. xi. 11, 12, xxvii. 13, where the ingathering of Israel to form a Messianic community is pictured. The eleventh echoes Isa. i. 26 : 'And I will restore thy judges as at the first, and thy counsellors as at the beginning.' The words 'and put away from us grief and sighing' must, as indicated, be a later insertion. 'Do Thou alone reign over us' recalls Mic. iv. 7. The thirteenth is a prayer for the righteous who will receive their reward in the Messianic time. The fourteenth Benediction clearly presupposes, in its present form, the destruction of the City ; it has been adapted to altered circumstances ; this is seen also in the Palestinian recension, but this latter still retains clear traces of its originally Messianic character, it runs : 'Have mercy, O Lord our God, upon us and upon Jerusalem Thy city, and upon Zion the dwelling-place of Thy glory, and upon the kingdom of the house of David Thy Messiah. Blessed art Thou, O Lord God of David, that buildest Jerusalem.'

Benediction xii does not concern us ; we have seen that it was added about A.D. 100. As to Benediction xv, Elbogen has shown conclusively that, as a separate Benediction, it found its way into the *Shemôneh 'Esreh* about the middle of the third century A.D., though some of the old rituals seem to point to its subject-matter having at one time formed part of

[1] *JE* xi. 281 *a*.

the fourteenth Benediction.[1] With Elbogen's facts and arguments in reference to the fifteenth Benediction we cannot deal here as this would take us too far afield.

An important fact about the *Shemôneh 'Esreh* which needs emphasis, although already referred to, is its illustration of the truth that the idea of prayer in the Jewish Liturgy connotes praise and thanksgiving as well as making petitions.[2] We have seen that the first three Benedictions are ascriptions of praise, and the last three expressions of thanksgiving, and that they form a framework within which the petitions are placed. Regarding these latter it is both interesting and important to bear in mind that they were not originally of a fixed character like the original six. Apart from the subject-matter the form of the words was left to the individual leader in prayer;[3] so that the earliest form of prayer, in the strict sense of petition, was *extempore*. They varied as occasion required; though, in course of time, they, too, became fixed.

(*c*) THE KEDÛSHAH. Attached to the third Benediction is what is called the *Kedûshah* ('Sanctification'). In its original form in the Liturgy there is every reason to believe that it consisted simply of the following:

'And one cried unto another, and said, Holy, holy, holy, is the Lord of hosts; the whole earth is full of His glory (Isa. vi. 3). Blessed be the glory of the Lord from His place' (Ezek. iii. 12).

---

[1] *Op. cit.*, pp. 39 ff., 52 ff.
[2] In the Old Testament thanksgiving and petition are embraced in the word *hithpallẹl*.
[3] Cp. Elbogen, *Op. cit.*, p. 2.

To this was added in the early stage of the history of the *Kedûshah* :

' The Lord shall reign for ever, thy God, O Zion, unto all generations. Praise ye the Lord ' (Ps. cxlvi. 10).

Other elements were added in course of time; but its present form of responses by the leader in prayer and the congregation echoes pre-Christian use.[1] ' It is highly probable ', says Dembitz, ' that the responsive *Kedûshah* in the modern sense is very old, and that it was known to Hillel and Shammai ; for it could not have been introduced later on without causing a dispute that would have left its traces in the Talmud.'[2] The echo of some such dispute seems, however, to occur in *Tosephta, Ber.* i. 9 : ' We do not respond together with him who pronounces the Benediction. [But] R. Judah used to respond together with him who pronounced the Benediction : *Holy, holy, holy, is the Lord of hosts, the whole earth is full of His glory*, and, *Blessed be the glory of the Lord from His place.* All the [words] R. Judah used to say together with him who pronounced the Benediction.'[3] The Rabbi mentioned lived during the first half of the second century A.D.

The importance of the *Kedûshah* is such that it occurs three times in different parts of the Liturgy ; its recitation after *Yôtzer* (see p. 47, above) is in all probability also pre-Christian.[4]

(*d*) THE 'ALENU PRAYER. This prayer which now concludes the daily Morning Service ('*Alenu* means ' It is meet for us ') belonged originally to the service for the New Year festival. Abrahams says that ' the

---

[1] *JE* vii. 463 *b*.   [2] Cp. Zunz, *Op. cit.*, p. 383.

[3] Lukyn Williams's edition. It is also spoken of in *Sopherim* xvii. 12.

[4] See further Zunz, *Op. cit.*, p. 382 ; Elbogen, *Op. cit.*, pp. 61 ff. ; Abrahams, *Op. cit.*, pp. xlvii ff., lx ff., lxxxii ff.

'*Alenu* Prayer, so named from its opening word, is very generally held to be pre-Christian in date. The whole congregation prostrated itself while confessing faith in the one God, and proclaiming the hope of the universal acceptance of the Divine Sovereignty.'[1] By some liturgical scholars this prayer is assigned to Rabbi Arika (usually known as 'Rab') about A.D. 230; but as Kohler says: 'Zunz and his followers—who ascribe the prayer to Rab, simply because in his school the Jewish Liturgy received its permanent form—disregarded the fact that it stands in no organic connexion with the rest of the New Year's prayer',[2] to which it became attached; and, as he says further, 'the omission of a personal Messiah from the expression of a Messianic hope points to a pre-Christian era; and the very title "King of the kings of kings"—found in Dan. ii. 37—shows that the formula used at the prostration goes back to Persian times when kings bore the title of King of Kings'; and he refers to Moses Mendelssohn's declaration that it is one of the oldest prayers of the nation, a proof of its age and pre-Christian character being 'the fact that no mention is made in it of the restoration of the Jewish Temple and state, which would scarcely have been omitted had it been composed after their destruction. It was obviously written at the time when the Jews still lived in their own land.'

The prayer consists of two parts; the following translation is from Dalman's text:[3]

It is meet that we should praise the Lord of all; that we should ascribe greatness to Him who formed (the world) from the beginning.

---

[1] *Studies in Pharisaism and the Gospels*, Second Series, p. 19 (1924).
[2] *JE* i. 337 *a*.   [3] *Op. cit.*, p. 307.

He made us not as the nations of (other) lands ; He placed us not as all the (other) families of the earth [lit. 'land'].

He hath not assigned unto us a portion as unto them ; nor our lot like unto (that of) all their multitude.

They worship vain things and emptiness ; they pray unto that which profiteth not.

We worship before the King of the kings of kings ; that stretcheth out the heavens and layeth the foundation of the earth.

The seat of His glory is in the heavens above ; and the abode of His strength is in the far off heights.

He is our God, and there is none other beside ; truly our King, and there is none but He.

Therefore we hope in Thee, O Lord our God ; that we may speedily see the glory of Thy might,

When Thou removest the abominations from the earth, and the idols shall be utterly cut off ;

When the world shall be set right in the Kingdom of the Almighty ; and all the children of flesh shall call upon Thy Name.

When Thou wilt turn unto Thyself all the wicked of the earth, that all the inhabitants of the world may perceive and know

That to Thee every knee must bow, every tongue swear.

Before Thee, O Lord our God, let them bow and fall down ; and to the glory of Thy great Name let them give honour.

And let them take upon themselves the yoke of Thy Kingdom, and do Thou reign over them for ever and ever.

For the Kingdom is Thine, and for ever and ever shalt Thou reign in glory.

VI. The Amen.

Judging from such passages as Ps. xli. 13, lxxii. 19, lxxxix. 52, cvi. 48, it is evident that the responsive 'Amen' came from the Temple Liturgy. But there is evidence that the congregational responsive formula was originally longer, for in the *Tosephta, Ber.* vii. 22, it is said : ' They did not answer "Amen" in the Temple. And whence do we know that they did not answer "Amen" in the Temple? Because it is said, *Stand up and bless the Lord your God for ever and ever* [Neh. ix. 5] ; and it says (then), *And let them bless Thy glorious Name, which is exalted above all blessing and praise,* above every single Blessing and above every single (ascription of) praise'; i. e. there is no mention of 'Amen'. Whether or not this was the case at some early period, it is certain from such a passage, e. g., as Ps. lxxxix. 52, *Blessed be the Lord for evermore, Amen and Amen,* that in the Temple Liturgy the 'Amen' was used, unless we are to assume that these two Amens are a later addition to the text, a possibility which is not excluded. However this may have been, there can be no doubt that this simple response was used in the Synagogue Liturgy from its first beginnings. When the *Shemôneh 'Esreh* was recited, for example, after the utterance of each benediction by the leader in prayer the congregation responded with 'Amen'. It was the same at the giving of the Priestly Blessing; after each sentence the people said 'Amen'.[1] So important was this response by the congregation considered, that in the large Synagogue in Alexandria, where there was a difficulty for all the members of the congregation to hear when the end of a prayer or a benediction was reached, an official stood up on the platform in the centre of the Synagogue and waved a flag as a sign to the congregation to make the response.[2]

---

[1] See Elbogen, *Op. cit.,* pp. 95 ff.

[2] *Ibid., BT, Sukkah* 51 *b.* Another instance is given in the Mishnah, *Ta'anith* ii. 5.

VII. KADDISH.

Kaddish means 'sanctification', and refers to the Name of God. The origin of this liturgical piece is to be sought in the words, 'May His great Name be blessed for ever and to all eternity.' This phrase was uttered by teachers at the conclusion of their discourses, and therefore had originally nothing to do with the Liturgy.

'It was a firmly rooted principle', says Elbogen, 'that discourses should conclude with a joyful looking forward to the Messianic future; but to these eschatological conclusions some teachers added a short prayer . . . one such prayer which in course of time became generally adopted was *Kaddish*. Its first sentence contains the two eschatological petitions for the sanctification of the divine Name and the coming of the Kingdom, and to these petitions belongs the eulogy, "May His great Name be blessed." . . . This is the kernel and the original meaning of Kaddish.' [1]

The antiquity of *Kaddish* (in its original form) is suggested, firstly, by the short and simple character of the eschatological petitions; secondly, by the fact that there is no reference to the destruction of the Temple (cp. the later addition to the seventeenth Benediction of the *Shemôneh 'Esreh*, p. 61, above); thirdly, by the further fact that, as we shall see later (pp. 151 ff.), there is some reason to believe that the identical thoughts in the first paragraph of *Kaddish* and the first three petitions of the Lord's Prayer point to a knowledge of it on the part of Christ; and fourthly, its home was Palestine, not Babylonia. [2]

---

[1] *Op. cit.*, p. 93; cp. Zunz, *Op. cit.*, p. 385, and see *Sopherim* xix (towards the end).

[2] See Elbogen, *Op. cit.*, p. 94.

Kaddish is written in Aramaic; but, as Elbogen points out, it is not the Aramaic dialect of the people, but bears the special idiom of the schools, and is known from the language of the officially recognized Targums.

In the Liturgy there are three forms of *Kaddish*, and there is also what is called 'Half-*Kaddish*' (i.e. the first half); it is only with this last that we are concerned; for this is the oldest part of *Kaddish*; its text in the ancient rituals varies much less than is the case with the latter half;[1] this points to antiquity. Half-*Kaddish* runs as follows:

Magnified and hallowed be His great Name in the world which He created according to His will.

May He establish His Kingdom in your life-time and in your days, and in the life-time of all the house of Israel speedily and in a near time. And say ye, Amen.

May His great Name be blessed for ever and to all eternity.

In the Liturgy *Kaddish* marks off the close of parts of the service, being parallel herein to the Lord's Prayer in the Anglican Liturgy.

VIII. PSALMS.

The liturgical use of psalms in the Jewish Church in pre-Christian times is too well known to need many words. The adaptation of the Temple Liturgy by the Synagogue took place while the Temple was still standing. The place of the psalms in the synagogal liturgy has undergone variation; the number in use is larger now than was originally the case; though even now only about half the psalms of the Psalter are used.

---

[1] See De Sola Pool, *The Old Jewish Aramaic Prayer, the Kaddish* (1909).

That part of the service which is now called *Zemirôth* ('Psalms') has its kernel in Pss. cxlv–cl; these are mentioned by Rabbi Jose ben Chalaphta (first half of the second century A. D.) as being said at the daily service in the Synagogue.[1]

Very ancient, and likewise part of the Temple Liturgy, was the special psalm for each day of the week. In the Mishnah, *Tamid* vii. 4, it is said: 'These were the psalms which the Levites used to recite in the Temple; on the first day of the week they used to recite *The earth is the Lord's* (xxiv); on the second day, *Great is the Lord* (xlviii); on the third day, *God standeth in the congregation of the mighty* (lxxxii); on the fourth day, *God of vengeance* (xciv); on the fifth day, *Exult aloud unto God our strength* (lxxxi); on the sixth day, *The Lord reigneth* (xciii); on the Sabbath, *A Psalm, a song for the Sabbath day* (xcii). It is a psalm and song also for the hereafter, for the day which will be wholly a Sabbath and a rest for life everlasting.'

In the Septuagint five of these psalms have inscriptions indicating the day to which they belong; in those for the third and fifth days this is wanting.

In the Mishnah, *Sukkah* iv. 5, it is recorded that in the Temple the liturgical psalms were sung in three parts, while *Tamid* vii. 3 tells of how the sons of Levi blew on trumpets after each part.

As to the proper psalms for festivals a good deal of information is given in the tractate *Sopherim*; e. g. xlvii was the proper psalm for *Rôsh-hashanah* (New Year's Day); lxxvi and cxviii. 25 to the end those for the Feast of Tabernacles; civ for New Moon festivals; cxxx for the Day of Atonement; and

---

[1] *Sopherim* xvii. 11.

others.[1] The Hallelujah Psalms, i. e. civ–cvi, cxi–cxiii, cxv–cxvii, cxxxv, cxlvi–cl, were known by heart by the people. There were, doubtless, many other parts of the service which the people knew by heart in days when they could not otherwise have taken their proper share in it. The passages in the New Testament in which speakers quote from the Psalms evidently point to their having been committed to memory (Lk. xx. 42, xxiv. 44 ; Acts i. 20, xiii. 33).[2]

' In the synagogues', says Rabbi Hirsch, ' the psalms were chanted antiphonally, the congregation repeating after every verse chanted by the precentor the first verse of the psalm in question. " Hallelujah " was the word with which the congregation was invited to take part in this chanting. Hence it originally prefaced the psalms, not, as in the Masoretic text, coming at the end. At the conclusion of the psalm the " Makre " or Precentor added a doxology ending with : 'and say ye Amen '; whereupon the congregation replied : " Amen, Amen ".' [3]

The Mishnah passages which speak of the psalms in worship refer to the Temple Liturgy only; we get next to no information from that source regarding their use in the Synagogue worship. This is to be explained by the fact that every one was so familiar with the subject that it required no mention. There is,

---

[1] See *Sopherim* xvii. 11, xviii. 2, xix. 2, and elsewhere. See also Thackeray, *Op. cit.*, Lect. ii.

[2] Much valuable information about the knowledge of the Old Testament Scriptures among the first Christians, and later, will be found in Harnack's *Über den privaten Gebrauch der heiligen Schriften in der alten Kirche* (1912).

[3] *JE* x. 247 *b*. For the psalms in the worship of the Synagogue, see further Oesterley, *The Psalms in the Jewish Church*, especially pp. 129 ff. (1910).

however, one exception; we are told that the Hallel Psalms (cxiii–cxviii) were used on eighteen days in the year at the end of *Shacharith* (Morning Service), and that there was a benediction known as *Birkath ha-Shir* which introduced or closed their recitation.[1]

IX. CONFESSION.

What are called the *Selichôth* (i.e. prayers for forgiveness; the word comes from the root *salach* 'to forgive') form an important element in the Jewish Liturgy. In their original form they were based on biblical texts such as 2 Sam. xxiv. 14; Isa. xx. 20, cxxxv; Dan. ix. 9 and others, and were used in the Temple Liturgy. But prayers for forgiveness only have their *raison d'être* when preceded by confession of sins. Accordingly forms of confession, based upon such passages as Ezra ix. 5 ff., x. 1, were a part of the Temple Liturgy which was taken over by the Synagogue. Following these there were 'petitions for grace' called *Tachanunim*. The order of this particular part of the service was thus: confession, prayer for forgiveness, prayer for grace. That this order is ancient receives interesting confirmation in the *Prayer of Manasses*, which is not later than the middle of the last pre-Christian century. There can be little doubt that this is a liturgical piece adapted to the apocryphal story of Manasses.[2] When analysed it will be found to follow the order just referred to. Thus, apart from the introductory ascription of praise and the concluding doxology, there is confession (verses 9–12); prayer for forgiveness (verse 13); prayer for grace (verse 14).

[1] Elbogen, *Op. cit.*, pp. 125, 249.

[2] See further Oesterley, *The Books of the Apocrypha*, pp. 407 ff (1914).

The shortness of each of these points to the antiquity of the piece, for in later days there was a constant tendency to prolong, especially the confession. This can be seen, e.g., in another Jewish Hellenistic work of later date, *Joseph and Asenath*, chap. xii; traces of the same order are, however, discernible; the confession and prayer for forgiveness are interwoven, and this is followed by the prayer for grace: 'And now I am an orphan and desolate, and I have no other hope save Thee, O Lord. . . . Have mercy upon me, Lord, and keep me pure and virgin . . .'

Forms for confession for daily use were provided; but it was the service for the Day of Atonement which contained forms for confession of sin of the most striking character. As is well known, the confession on this day was originally made by the high-priest on behalf of all the people (Lev. xvi. 21). On this the Mishnah, *Yoma* iii. 8, says: 'And the priest [i.e. the high-priest] stood at the east, with his face westwards, and pressed his two hands upon it [i.e. the goat], and made confession (*hithwadda*); and thus did he speak, O God [lit. Name], I have done iniquity, I have transgressed, I have sinned, before Thee, I and my house. . . . And they responded after him, Blessed be the Name of the glory of His Kingdom for ever and ever.' The second confession is described in iv. 2, in very similar terms. The essence of the confession consists in the words, 'I have done iniquity, I have transgressed, I have sinned' (עָוִיתִי פָּשַׁעְתִּי חָטָאתִי), and this is the basis of the later and more elaborate forms of confession. Of these the earliest mentioned in the Mishnah are spoken of by authorities who lived early in the third century A.D. and onwards; but these forms of confession were so well known that they are only referred to by their initial words; so that even as fixed forms of confession there must be a long history behind them. But there are earlier authorities, of the Tannaitic period (the first two centuries of the Christian era), who speak of a form of confession incorporated in the *Shemôneh 'Esreh* for the Day of Atonement.[1]

Three liturgical pieces which are preserved in the modern Jewish Prayer Book, and which in one form or another occur in all the ancient rituals, deserve a few words of special notice because in their original form they go back, in all probability, to pre-Christian times.

The first is the form of confession called *Ashamnu* ('We have trespassed'), which is introduced by a short piece ending with: '. . . but we, even we, have sinned'. This last is the title of the confession mentioned by Mar Samuel[2] (first half of the third century A.D.). *Ashamnu* is an alphabetical confession, said by the congregation, in which particular sins are enumerated. Its text is practically identical in all the ancient rituals; Elbogen thinks that in its present form it dates from the fifth century A.D.

Another form which is quoted by name by Abba Arika (first half of the third century A.D., he died in 247) is as follows: '*Thou knowest the secrets of eternity*, and the hidden mysteries of all living. Thou searchest the recesses of the inner parts [*lit.* the belly], and triest the reins and the heart. Nothing is concealed from Thee, and nothing is hidden from before Thine eyes. May it, therefore, be Thy will, O Lord our God and the God of our fathers, to forgive us all our sins, to blot out for us all our iniquities, and to grant us remission for all our transgressions.' The shortness of this piece

[1] Elbogen, *Op. cit.*, pp. 149 ff.
[2] *BT, Yoma* 87 *b* (Elbogen).

does not permit of its having gone through much alteration.

This is followed by what must be the most searching form of confession of sins in any Liturgy; it is known as '*Al Chēt* ('For the sin') from the two opening words, and contains a very long-drawn-out enumeration of every imaginable sin. Originally it was very much shorter as can be seen by its form in the old rituals; in that of Amram it consists of only eight sentences; but this may be an abbreviated form. From some parts of it one sees at once that it goes, in part, back to the time of the Temple Service; e.g. 'And for the sins for which we owe an offering, varying according to our means . . .'

On the general subject of confession in the Jewish Liturgy, see further Dukes, *Zur Kenntniss der Neuhebräischen religiösen Poesie*, pp. 32 ff. (1842); *JE* vii. 498 ff., and especially, xi. 170 ff.; Abrahams, *Festival Studies*, chap. iv (1906); *SLRJ*, pp. 179 ff.

X. KIDDÛSH.

Kiddûsh ('Sanctification') is, and was, a weekly ceremony which ushers in the Sabbath. It is a sanctifying of the day, hence its name. Originally a home ceremony it became transferred, in course of time, to the Synagogue; and it was celebrated both in the home and in the Synagogue; this is the case at the present day. It forms, therefore, a part of the Jewish Liturgy.

As to its antiquity there can be no doubt. It is referred to as a well-known ceremony in the Mishnah by Rabbis who lived quite at the beginning of the first century A.D.[1] According to the Talmud (*Berakhôth*

[1] See further below, p. 170.

33 *a*) 'the origin of the *Kiddûsh* can be traced to the time of the Great Synagogue ',[1] i. e. traditionally to the time of Ezra. This may or may not be a trustworthy tradition; but we have stronger evidence for its antiquity. As Dembitz says: 'From the controversies between the schools of Shammai and Hillel on various points connected with the *Kiddûsh*, it is clearly seen that the ceremony is very old.' Shammai and Hillel, and their respective 'schools' were already in existence before the time of Christ. Their controversies about various points in connexion with *Kiddûsh* which inaugurated the Sabbath, and *Habdalah*[2] which concluded it, show that quite at the beginning of the Christian era both ceremonies must have been long in existence.[3] But perhaps the most convincing evidence for the antiquity of *Kiddûsh* is to be seen in the practical identity of its text as preserved in all the ancient rituals. 'The text of *Kiddûsh*', says Elbogen, 'is, but for minor details, identical in all the copies, a proof that it rests on sound tradition.'[4] The tenacity with which religious customs are clung to is sufficiently well known to need any further emphasis here; but the fact is worth bearing in mind in this connexion. All authorities are agreed that the ceremony of *Kiddûsh* was a well-established institution before the beginning of the Christian era. We shall have to say a good deal more about it below (pp. 170 ff.), so that it will be well to give the text of it here in its Passover form:

[1] Dembitz in *JE* vii. 483 *b*.

[2] The word means 'separation', i.e. of the Sabbath from ordinary days.

[3] E.g. in the Mishnah, *Berakhôth* vii, viii, and in *Tosephta, Ber.* iii. 8, vi. 1, 2, 5; see Lukyn Williams's translation, *Tractate Berakôth*, for these references (1921); and see also the tractate *Pesachim* x. 2.

[4] *Op. cit.*, p. 112.

And it was evening and it was morning, the sixth day.

And the heavens and the earth and all the host of them were finished.

And on the seventh day God finished His work which He had done, and He rested on the seventh day from all His work which He had done. And God blessed the seventh day, and hallowed it, for He rested on it from all His work which God had created and made.

[The words said over the cup] ' Blessed art Thou, O Lord our God, King Eternal, who createst the fruit of the vine.'

Blessed art Thou, O Lord our God, King Eternal, who hast chosen us from all peoples, and hast exalted us above all tongues, and has sanctified us by Thy commandments. And Thou hast given us in love, O Lord our God, Sabbaths for rest, and appointed times for gladness, festivals and seasons for joy : this Sabbath day and this feast of Unleavened Bread, the season of our freedom.

Blessed art Thou, O Lord our God, King Eternal, who hast kept us alive, and hast preserved us, and enabled us to reach this season.

[The words said over the bread] ' Blessed art Thou, O Lord our God, King Eternal, who bringest forth bread from the earth.'

XI. THE DECALOGUE.

It is interesting to notice that the liturgical recitation of the Decalogue is attested by both Talmuds as having been at one time customary in the Synagogue. It formed part of the liturgical recitation of the *Shema'*, but was later discontinued for anti-Christian reasons. Thus, in the Jerusalem Talmud, *Berakhôth* i. 8, it is said : 'Of right they should read the Ten Words every day. And on account of what do they not read them ? On account of the cavilling of the heretics (*Minim*), so that they might not say, These only were given to Moses on Sinai.' Again, in Babylonian Talmud, *Ber.* 12 *a*, we read : 'And they read the Ten Words, and the *Shema'* [reference is then made to some other liturgical pieces, and the passage continues]: ' Rab Jehudah said, and Shemuel said, In the provinces also they sought to read them, but they had already stopped them because of the murmuring of the heretics (*Minim*).'[1] The Decalogue is also mentioned as an integral part of the Liturgy in the Mishnah, *Tamid* v. 1 ; and the Nash Papyrus,[2] a liturgical fragment belonging to the second or third century A.D., contains the *Shema'* and the Decalogue.

It is thus quite clear that the recitation of the Ten Commandments formed an integral part of the *Shema'*, and was at one time recited daily in the Temple, and later in the Synagogue. It can, therefore, hardly be doubted that the earliest Jewish Christians would have used this form (*Shema'* and Decalogue) in their worship.

. . . .

These, then, are the elements in the Jewish Liturgy which may be regarded with reasonable certainty as being pre-Christian. They include all the more important parts of that Liturgy. It is probable that there are other pieces which date from pre-Christian times ; but these have been omitted because the *data* are insufficient to prove this.

---

[1] Quoted by Taylor, *Sayings of the Jewish Fathers*, pp. 119 ff. (1897).

[2] On this see S. A. Cooke in the *Proceedings* of the Society of Bibl. Arch., xxv, pp. 34 ff. (1903).

PART II

JEWISH LITURGICAL INFLUENCE
ON EARLY FORMS
OF CHRISTIAN WORSHIP

III

WORSHIP IN THE EARLY CHRISTIAN COMMUNITIES

It is not intended to attempt to give, even in outline, an account of the constitution and organization of the early Christian communities; that would be outside the scope of the present inquiry; but it is necessary to take note of some facts regarding those communities which may throw direct or indirect light on the special subject we have in hand.

I

The first thing which must soon strike every investigator here is the meagreness of the *data* of a direct kind which might give information concerning details of worship. The absence of such *data* is, from the present point of view, an argument in favour of the general contention of this chapter, viz. that the influence of the Jewish Liturgy was very marked on the earliest forms of Christian worship ; for if the mode of worship to which the earliest Christians were accustomed had been altered we might reasonably expect some mention of it as being something new, and, as a matter of fact, the one respect in which the accustomed mode of worship *did* differ from the traditional use is given very pointed mention ; but if the accustomed mode of worship was continued the fact would be so natural and in the ordinary course of things as not to require anything further than an occasional reference. This silence, therefore, quite apart from other arguments, in itself

offers some justification for the belief that the earliest
Christians continued to worship in their traditional
way. The New Testament *indicates* what this traditional way was, but gives very few details as to its
form; for these, as we have seen in the previous
chapter, we have to go elsewhere. Nevertheless, it is
necessary to draw attention to the indications given in
the New Testament, although the ground to be covered
in doing so is very familiar, both because they will
show that the foundation upon which our superstructure
is to be built is a sound one, whatever views may be
taken regarding some of the details of the superstructure
itself; and also because without entering into the Jewish
atmosphere of the New Testament, and especially of
the Gospels, it is impossible to render justice to many
of the points to be discussed in later chapters.

While it is nowhere directly asserted in the Gospels
that our Lord took part in the Temple worship it is
difficult to believe that He did not do so. Prof. Bartlet,
in writing about forms of worship in the New Testament, says that

'here the main fact is that Jesus' own example and
teaching are associated with the synagogal type of
worship rather than with the Temple, the seat of the
sacrificial and priestly system of worship. For to Him
the Temple was primarily "a house of prayer", and
that private (Lk. xviii. 10) rather than public prayer.
Indeed the latter hardly seems to be alluded to by
Jesus at all (not even in Matt. xviii. 19). His teaching
on worship is mainly on genuine prayer, as opposed to
formal prayers, "vain repetitions" (Matt. vi. 5 ff., cp.
Lk. xviii. 10–14); and even "the Lord's Prayer" is
given as an example of prayer of the right sort rather
than as a form for regular repetition.'[1]

[1] *ERE* xii. 763 *b*.

We agree that the synagogal type of worship set the pattern for the worship of the early Church, though we think that this can only apply *in part* to the Eucharist; for there were in the sacrificial worship of the Temple certain underlying principles and truths which hold good whether sacrifices are offered or not. But Prof. Bartlet's words seem to the present writer a little one-sided. Christ's daily presence in the Temple during the period of His sojourn in Jerusalem for the purpose of teaching is mentioned several times (Matt. xxi. 55, xxvi. 55; Mk. xiv. 49; Lk. xix. 47, xxii. 53; Jn. xviii. 20; cp. Matt. xxi. 23 ff.); it is in the highest degree improbable that He would be present there only for teaching and withdraw during the times of worship. Had that been the case His enemies would not have been backward in reproaching Him with this neglect; the Gospels, which indicate so clearly other accusations against Him, would not have been silent regarding this one had there been anything to record. If Christ went to Jerusalem to attend the Jewish feasts, particularly the Passover, would not His presence imply that He sanctioned the sacrificial worship, at any rate as regards the Passover lamb? In the fourth Gospel, which in some respects preserves a more accurate tradition than the Synoptists, we have a long account of His presence there during the Feast of Tabernacles (vii. 20–44). Then, again, in regard to what Prof. Bartlet says as to our Lord's teaching on prayer, he does not seem to have taken all the facts into consideration. If, as he says, Christ's own example and teaching were associated with 'the synagogal type of worship', then He must assuredly have countenanced forms of prayer for regular repetition; for, to take but one example, the most important prayer of the synagogal Liturgy, the *Shemôneh*

'*Esreh*, was regularly repeated thrice daily. Of our Lord Himself we are told in Matt. xxvi. 39–44 how He prayed; in verse 44 we read that He 'prayed a third time, saying again the same words' (cp. Mk. xiv. 32 ff.). As to the Lord's Prayer being 'an example of prayer of the right sort rather than a form for regular repetition', we would point out that, in Lk. xi. 2, Christ says to His disciples, '*When* ye pray, say . . .'; does this not suggest a regular habit? If so, then the Lord's Prayer must have been regularly repeated by the disciples; and it was done at the Lord's command.[1]

However, with the proviso mentioned above, and remembering that the synagogal Liturgy was taken over from that of the Temple, we agree with Prof. Bartlet that Christ was more associated with the synagogal type of worship than with that of the Temple. For our present purpose it is especially important to note the many references in the Gospels to Christ's presence in the Synagogue. If in the majority of cases it is to His *teaching* in the Synagogue to which reference is made, it must be remembered that the chief occasions for teaching there were provided for during divine service after the reading from the Scriptures; and Lk. iv. 16 ff., a passage about which we shall have more to say later, gives the clearest proof and illustration of our Lord's practice; for it is quite obviously divine service, and not merely

---

[1] Heiler says truly and beautifully : 'The offering up of prayer on the part of Jesus is, just like His joyful message of a loving Father and of the coming Kingdom of God, the creation of something that was new (ein schöpferisch Neues); but this new creation is, nevertheless, woven into the old forms of piety and into the religious conceptions of the Jewish people' (*Das Gebet*, p. 240 [5th edition, 1923]).

a casual visit to the synagogue, to which reference is here made.[1]

Over and over again we read of Christ's presence in the synagogue both on ordinary week-days and on the Sabbath.   To give but a few instances : in Matt. iv. 23 we read, 'And Jesus went about in all Galilee, teaching in their synagogues', cp. ix. 35, xiii. 54 ;   Mk. i. 39. Again, in Matt. xii. 9, 'And He departed thence and went into their synagogue', cp. Mk. iii. 1 ; Lk. vi. 6; in Mk. i. 21 it says, 'And they go into Capernaum ; and straightway on the Sabbath He entered into the synagogue and taught', cp. Lk. iv. 16, 44, xiii. 14 ; similarly in Mk. vi. 2, 'And when the Sabbath was come, He began to teach in the synagogue'; and once more, Jn. vi. 59, 'These things said He in the synagogue', and Jn. xviii. 20, 'I ever taught in synagogues, and in the Temple'.   This last passage points to a more frequent presence in the Temple than might be gathered from the Synoptic accounts.

Christ's practice was followed by the Apostles ; some passages illustrating this may be given.   Immediately after the Ascension it is said that the disciples 'returned to Jerusalem with great joy, and were continually in the Temple, blessing God', Lk. xxiv. 52, 53.   That they attended the daily worship in the Temple seems at least implied in Acts ii. 46, 'And day by day, continuing stedfastly with one accord in the Temple, and breaking bread at home . . .'; and again in Acts iii. 1, 'Now Peter and John were going up into the Temple at the hour of prayer, being the ninth hour', cp. iv. 2, v. 12, 20, 21, 25, 42, xxi. 26, 39, xxii. 3, xxiv. 8.

---

[1] We do not, of course, mean to imply by this that every reference to Christ's presence in the synagogue meant that He was there during divine service.

But it was, of course, mainly in the synagogues that the preaching and teaching activity of the apostles was exhibited; and in the *Acts* we have abundant record of this. To cite all the passages would be tedious; but the following summary may be offered.

One or other of the apostles, though the records refer mainly to St. Paul, are spoken of as ministering the word in the synagogue at the following places: Damascus (ix. 20), Salamis (xiii. 5), Antioch in Pisidia (xiii. 14, 15), this is an important passage, for it tells us quite definitely that the apostles were taking part in the Sabbath service: 'And they went into the synagogue on the Sabbath day and sat down. And after the reading of the Law and the Prophets the rulers of the synagogue sent unto them, saying, Brethren, if ye have any word of exhortation for the people, say on.' Further, Iconium (xiv. 1). In xv. 21 St. James speaks of 'Moses', i.e. the Pentateuchal lesson, being 'read in the synagogues every Sabbath' (cp. 2 Cor. iii. 14, 15), clearly implying the presence there of those whom he was addressing. At Thessalonica, 'where was a synagogue of the Jews', St. Paul, 'as his custom was, went in unto them, and for three Sabbath days reasoned with them from the Scriptures' (xvii. 2). Again, Berœa (xvii. 10), Athens (xvii. 17), Corinth (xviii. 4), Ephesus (xviii. 19, 26, xix. 8).

From these passages we can see the importance which the apostles attached to the synagogue and its services. It is only incidentally that the Sabbath is mentioned as the day on which they went there; but though they were doubtless often in the synagogues on week-days, we may reasonably assume that the Sabbath day services were especially made use of for preaching the word there; for on those occasions there would be

the largest number of listeners, and the opportunity
granted to any man of speaking to the assembled worshippers after the reading of the Law or the Prophets,
or after each, was one which the apostles would have
been eager to seize.

So far, then, it may be claimed that the evidence of
the New Testament makes it certain that the earliest
Christian communities continued the traditional mode
of worship to which they had been accustomed in the
synagogue.   That traditional form of worship had
naturally become endeared to them, and, *as far as it
went*, it satisfied their spiritual needs; that is proved
by their continued observance of it.   So that when the
time came, as it evidently soon did, for these early
Christian communities to construct a liturgy of their
own, it would be the most natural thing in the world
for them to be influenced by the form and thought of
their traditional liturgy with which they were so familiar.
And we should expect to find the marks of that influence
in the early liturgy of the Church.

II

But the New Testament passages referred to, which
tell us of the apostles worshipping in the synagogue,
only present us with one side of the picture.   There
are other passages, of even greater importance, which
tell us of another and additional mode of worship, which
differed in place, time, and form from the traditional
services.   While the worship in the synagogue was of
a more or less formal character, this other mode of
worship appears as informal.   But here too, as we
shall hope to show in later chapters, the influence of
the synagogue is to be discerned.

These passages must be briefly considered, although the ground to be covered is very familiar; but it is absolutely necessary that they should receive some attention in dealing with the worship of the first Christian communities.

First, as to the *place* of worship. In Acts i. 12–14 we read of the apostles going up to 'the upper chamber, where they were abiding'; they are joined by some women, including 'Mary the mother of Jesus, and His brethren'; here 'with one accord they continued stedfastly in prayer'. This is the record of an act of informal worship at which, it may reasonably be assumed, the leader in prayer prayed extempore. The upper chamber may well have been the scene of the Last Supper, but on this occasion there was no Eucharist; at any rate, no mention is made of the breaking of bread. In Acts ii. 1 ff., the account of the descent of the Spirit on the Day of Pentecost, we are told that the same company were all together 'in one place'; this was a house, as the next verse tells us. Probably it was the same house as that to which St. Peter and St. John came after their appearance before the Sanhedrin, described in Acts iv. 5 ff.; here, 'when they had prayed, the place was shaken wherein they were gathered together, and they were all filled with the Holy Ghost. . . .' Again, in Acts xii. 12 another place of meeting is referred to, 'the house of Mary the mother of John whose surname was Mark'; here 'many were gathered together and were praying'. A place of meeting, not specified, is spoken of in xiii. 1. Other places are 'the house of a certain man named Titus Justus'; this was in Corinth (xviii. 7, 8); the house of some brethren in Ptolemais (xxi. 7); the house of Philip the evangelist in Caesarea (xxi. 8). St. Paul,

when in Ephesus, tells how he had taught both publicly
and 'from house to house' (xx. 20). And, once more,
when he was in confinement in his own hired dwelling
in Rome, the people came to him there, and he preached
to them and taught them (xxviii. 23 ff.).[1]

Thus it was customary in the Dispersion as well as
in Jerusalem for the first Christians to hold informal
services in private houses, in addition to the liturgical
services in the synagogues.

Some indications are given as to what these services
consisted of. As we have seen, prayer was offered
on these occasions; and judging from the stress laid
on this it is evident that prayer was the most important
element; see, in addition to the passages already mentioned, Acts i. 24, 25, iv. 24, 31, xii. 12; 1 Cor. xiv. 16.
It has been pointed out (p. 52) that the characteristic of the ancient synagogal prayers was that they
included praise and thanksgiving. It is, therefore,
interesting to note that these elements are mentioned
in connexion with these informal services. Praise,
thanksgiving, and psalms or hymns are referred to in
Acts ii. 47, iv. 24 ff.; 1 Cor. xiv. 26 f.; Col. iii. 16;
Eph. v. 9. In addition, teaching and preaching are
mentioned in Acts xx. 7 f., xxviii. 23, 31; 1 Cor. xiv.
26 ff., and they are implied in other passages. The
last passage referred to shows us particularly that there
was no stereotyped form of service in this worship in
private houses; everything seems to have been left
to individual initiative. Nevertheless, there is reason
to believe, as we shall see later, that, so far as the
prayers were concerned, although the leader in prayer
might use his own words, the subject-matter was in
essence that of the liturgical prayers of the synagogue;

---

[1] See also Rom. xvi. 5; 1 Cor. xvi. 19; Col. iv. 15; Philemon 2.

indeed, it is probable that not only words of special import, but also whole phrases were adopted from these.

Finally, there are, apart from the Gospels, five passages in which the 'breaking of bread' is referred to.[1] Although the mention of this is so rare, two of these passages, at least, quite obviously imply that the 'breaking of bread' was of frequent occurrence.

The first of these is Acts ii. 42 : 'And they continued stedfastly in the apostles' teaching and fellowship, in the breaking of bread[2] and the prayers.' The reference is to the three thousand souls who had received the word from St. Peter, and had been baptized. The words 'they continued stedfastly' suggest that the passage was written some considerable time after ; so, too, the description of the religious manner of life of this large body. Therefore it points to what had become habitual. As no details are given concerning these four fundamental matters the implication is that they were familiar ; moreover, 'the prayers' suggest that they were well known.

This applies, too, to the next passage (Acts ii. 46), and receives emphasis from the fact that a considerable

---

[1] This does not mean to say that it is not *implied* in some other passages. On the other hand, the phrase occurs in Acts xxvii. 35, where it would seem that it refers to ordinary eating.

[2] Whether the 'breaking of bread' here refers to the Eucharist or the *Agapé* (as some hold, e. g. Spitta, *Urchristenthum*, i. 289) does not really much matter, for in these early days they were not separated, one implied the other. The Vulgate rendering of the passage, . . . *et in communicatione fractionis panis*, may be safely regarded as erroneous ; the Greek plainly presents two couplets which respectively belong together ; teaching and fellowship : breaking of bread and the prayers, the former representing in some sense practical religion, the latter devotional religion.

lapse of time clearly intervened (see verses 43–5) between the events recorded in the context both of this passage and the preceding one mentioned. It runs : 'And day by day continuing stedfastly with one accord in the Temple, and breaking of bread at home, they did take their food with gladness and singleness of heart, praising God, and having favour with all the people.' There will be differences of opinion regarding the allusions in this pregnant passage. We venture to offer the following interpretation : the 'continuing day by day in the Temple' refers to the daily services there ; the 'breaking of bread at home' refers to the weekly celebration of the Eucharist in private houses ; the taking 'their food with gladness and singleness of heart' refers to the *Agapé*, rendered possible for all, poor as well as rich, through their having all things common (mentioned in the preceding context).

The third passage, Acts xx. 7–11 (especially the first and last verses), speaks of the breaking of bread 'upon the first day of the week' ; and the words imply again that the ceremony referred to was something familiar and customary : 'And upon the first day of the week, when we were gathered together to break bread . . .' This takes place in 'the upper chamber'; it is in a house in Troas where St. Paul 'tarried seven days'.

In our next passage, 1 Cor. x. 15–17, St. Paul puts a question to his hearers (to which an affirmative answer is obviously supposed) which shows that the service of the 'breaking of bread' was not only of frequent and regular occurrence, but that its inner meaning was familiar to them. 'I speak as to wise men ; judge ye what I say. The cup of blessing which we bless, is it not a communion of the blood of Christ? The bread which we break, is it not a communion of the body of Christ? seeing that we, who are many, are one bread, one body: for we all partake of the one bread.'

The last passage is 1 Cor. xi. 20–34. The observance of the ceremony is represented as so well known that familiarity has had the effect of obscuring the essence of the rite among the Corinthians; so much so that St. Paul has to remind them of this by recalling the details of its original institution. An important point in this passage regarding the organization of the Church is that the service is now celebrated (at any rate in Corinth) in some more or less public place of assembly; 'What, have ye not houses to eat and to drink in? or despise ye the church (better "congregation") of God?' See also verses 20, 22, 33. The regularity and frequency of the rite are implied in the words: 'As often as ye eat this bread . . .'

As we are here only dealing with forms of worship among the early Christian communities we do not touch upon the various other important questions raised by these passages. The only exception is the subject of the *Agapé*; but to this a separate chapter will be devoted.

III

We find, then, that the earliest Christians observed three forms of worship. There was the traditional Jewish form which was offered in the Temple; but as it was only those who lived in Jerusalem who could take regular part in it, it was, from the present point of view, of less importance than the Synagogue worship. This service was of a formal character; a certain amount of latitude was, however, permitted. It took place twice certainly, three times possibly, a day; but the Sabbath day services were of greater importance. Secondly, there seem to have been meetings in private houses for the purpose mainly of prayer (see, for example, Acts i. 12–14, iv. 5 ff., xii. 12, xx. 7 ff.); the procedure at these meetings was clearly quite informal; indeed, we are, perhaps, not justified in speaking of these as services; in any case, they were of a private character. And, thirdly, there was the specifically Christian service of the 'breaking of bread'. This also took place in private houses; though, judging from 1 Cor. xi. 20 ff., some development is discernible already in St. Paul's time regarding the place of meeting. This service was held on the first day of the week, so far as we can gather from the available evidence (see Acts xx. 7; 1 Cor. xvi. 2; Rev. i. 10).

The observance of these forms of worship of the earliest Christian communities is spoken of in Acts ii. 46: 'And day by day continuing stedfastly with one accord in the Temple, and breaking bread at home . . .'; and again in Acts v. 42: 'And every day in the Temple, and at home, they ceased not to teach and to preach Jesus as the Christ.' The Synagogue, of course, took the place of the Temple outside of Jerusalem; but it is probable that in Jerusalem, too, the services of the Synagogue as well as those of the Temple were attended by the apostles and their followers. And it is interesting to note that we have evidence that the Temple Liturgy was used in the Synagogue while the Temple was still in existence. Joshuah ben Chananiah,[1] one of the most prominent pupils of Jochanan ben Zakkai (see *Aboth* ii. 9), 'who had served in the sanctuary as

[1] He died A.D. 130.

a member of the Levitical choir (Bab. Talm. *Arakhin*
11 *b*), told how the choristers went in a body to the
Synagogue from the orchestra by the altar (Bab. Talm.
Sukka 53 *a*) and so participated in both services.'[1]
It is, of course, quite possible that the reference here
is to the Synagogue within the Temple precincts which
is spoken of in the Mishnah (*Yoma* vii. 1 ; *Sotah* vii.
7, 8); though it is well known that many other synagogues existed in Jerusalem at this time.[2]

Thus the first Christians offered up the same prayers
that all pious Jews did, visited the Temple for worship,
and doubtless offered sacrifices there like other Jews—
if they had not done so some indication of the fact
would surely have been forthcoming in the Acts—
attended the Synagogue, kept the Sabbath, and observed
the festivals (cp. St. Paul's anxiety to be in Jerusalem
in time for Pentecost, Acts xx. 16).

The indications of a separate organization and
government, independent of the Jewish Church, discernible from the earliest times (see Matt. xvi. 19,
xviii. 15 ff. ; John xx. 23; Acts v. 1 ff.) clearly did not
involve withdrawal from the Temple or Synagogue
worship. The two organizations existed side by side,
the Christian one being only supplementary. Acts ii.
41, 42 presents the picture of a community of which
worship formed the most important visible bond of
union : baptism, breaking of bread, apostolic teaching,
and prayers. Under the latter we are justified, by the
type of prayer found in the earliest forms of Christian
worship, in believing that, in addition to the Lord's

---

[1] F. L. Cohen in the *Jewish Encycl.* ix. 120 *a*.

[2] In the Jer. Talm. *Megilla* iii. 1 it is said that there were 480
synagogues in Jerusalem (Schürer, *Geschichte des Jüdischen Volkes*,
ii. 495, 524 [1907]).

Prayer, there were included such as the apostles and their disciples had always been in the habit of offering. The incidental notice in Acts vi. 7 ('. . . and a great company of the priests were obedient to the faith') is worth bearing in mind in this connexion.

The Hellenistic Jews of Palestine who had synagogues of their own (Acts vi. 9) would have used, in the main, the same form of worship as the Palestinian Jews, using, it may be supposed, the Greek language instead of Hebrew (or Aramaic in the case of one or two prayers, see pp. 49, 73). The first time we hear of any differences between Palestinian Jewish Christians and Gentile Jewish Christians (Acts xv. 1–39) they have nothing to do with worship. So far as the earliest periods are concerned it is striking to notice how, in spite of a marked divergence of views on some matters, the Jewish Christians in Jerusalem superintend and direct the Gentile missions. It is they who send forth Barnabas to Antioch (Acts xi. 22), who commission Judas and Silas to go there (Acts xv. 22), as well as Cephas (Gal. ii. 11) and others (Gal. ii. 12), whose authority is recognized by the Gentile Christians not only of Antioch, but also of Syria and Cilicia generally (Acts xv. 23, 31),[1] cp. also 1 Thess. ii. 14.

It is natural to assume that if the supremacy of the Jerusalem leaders was thus recognized and their directions followed by the Gentile Christian world beyond Palestine in the important matters dealt with in these passages, their example and practice would have been equally authoritative regarding the form and manner of worship. They had been the closest followers of Christ and had been guided by Him in all

---

[1] Note also St. Paul's solicitude for the poor saints in Jerusalem, 1 Cor. xvi. 1 3 ; cp. Acts xxiv. 17.

things. And here it is important to remember that Christ's attitude regarding such questions as Sabbath observance, ritual customs, and His teaching on the Law—and it was just on legal questions that differences arose between the Jerusalem leaders and the Gentile converts—did not touch upon the worship of the Synagogue. Regarding such things as prayer and fasting, it was not so much the matter, as the manner, to which Christ took objection.

There was nothing in the central elements of the worship of the Synagogue—the reading of the Scriptures, the discourse based on this, the prayers, the saying or singing of psalms, even the *Shema'* and its benedictions—in which Palestinian and Gentile Christians could not join.

We have, therefore, grounds for believing that during the period covered by the New Testament records Palestinian Jewish Christians as well as the Hellenistic Jewish and Gentile converts in the Dispersion used the Jewish liturgical form of worship in the Synagogue on Sabbaths and ordinary week-days, held their informal prayer-meetings in private houses, and on the first day of the week held a special form of worship of which the essential and central part was the 'breaking of bread'—the Eucharist—this being celebrated at first in the home, but even in these early days at some central place of meeting, occasionally.

Very little knowledge, however, regarding the details of the worship of these early Christian communities is to be gained from the New Testament. The first certain indications of these in Christian literature appear in the early part of the second century, when some fixed elements are seen to exist which are apparently firmly established and must therefore have been in use for some time. But this is not until the Christian Church had been finally severed from the Jewish. There is, therefore, a period of half a century at the very least during which we are in almost complete darkness as to the details of the worship of the early Christian communities, so far as our knowledge from Christian sources is concerned. Our early second-century information from these sources, however, justifies us in believing that what happened during this 'dark' period was this : the influence of Palestinian Jewish Christianity on Gentile Christianity had been sufficiently strong to induce the latter not only to adopt from the former the main elements of the synagogal worship, but also, after the final severance of the Jewish and Christian Churches and the consequent cessation of attendance at the Synagogue, to transfer much of the Sabbath Synagogue worship to the specific eucharistic service on the first day of the week.

To establish this contention, the first step has been taken, namely, to determine those elements in the synagogal liturgy which were already in existence at the beginning of the Christian era. We have next, after a brief consideration of the earliest Christian sources of information, to examine the earliest forms of Christian worship available and compare them with the pre-Christian elements of the Synagogue Liturgy. We shall then see in what respects the early Christian Liturgy has been influenced by that of the Synagogue.

IV

SOURCES FOR THE EARLIEST FORMS OF CHRISTIAN WORSHIP

A BRIEF enumeration of the earliest sources from which *data* are to be gathered regarding the elements of Christian worship in its beginnings is our next step. Details of what these sources offer will be given later so that a comparison may be made between these details and those of Jewish liturgical worship. At present we are only concerned with a bird's-eye view of the Christian sources, together with their approximate dates and places of origin. A selected bibliography for the texts of the sources, translations, &c., is added in the foot-notes.

As every liturgical investigator knows, a considerable difficulty presents itself in the fact that the earliest sources give, comparatively, so little direct evidence; and where this occurs it is only in regard to individual liturgical elements; it is not until the fourth century that a full view of the whole Liturgy can be gained, whereas our concern is, in the main, with the earlier centuries. However, the direct evidence, small as it is, will be found to be sufficient, we believe, for our central purpose. The indirect evidence of some of these earliest sources, moreover, is not to be despised; in the light of later liturgical developments, we may justifiably draw some inferences from them which bear upon the present investigation.

I

(*a*) Our earliest source is, of course, the *New Testament*. Some reference has already been made in the previous chapter to this source, and it will be dealt with again; it is, therefore, unnecessary to say anything further here excepting that the evidence is partly Palestinian, and partly from centres, both Jewish and Gentile, outside of Palestine.

(*b*) Our next source is the *First Epistle of Clement*,[1] belonging to about the year A.D. 96. This letter was written from the Church of Rome to the Church of Corinth. As will be seen, we have at the end of this epistle an extremely valuable piece of evidence concerning the form and content of prayer in the first beginnings of a Christian Liturgy.

(*c*) The *Epistle of Barnabas*[2] is not, it is true, of much help in the present investigation. But it offers here and there some details of interest. Who wrote this epistle, where it was written, and to whom it was written, are questions which cannot be answered owing to insufficiency of *data*; but from internal evidence it is agreed by most scholars that it was written at the end of the first, or beginning of the second century. It is largely a polemic against the Jewish interpretation of the Old Testament, and thus witnesses to the separation between the Jewish and Christian Churches as having already taken place.

[1] Gebhardt, Harnack, and Jahn, *Patrum Apostolicorum opera* (Editio minor), pp. 1 ff. (1877); Lightfoot, *The Apostolic Fathers*, Part I, vol. ii, pp. 5 ff. (1890); Funk, *Die apostolischen Väter*, pp. 33 ff. (1901); Kirsopp Lake, *The Apostolic Fathers*, i, pp. 8 ff. (in Loeb's Classical Library, 1912).

[2] Gebhardt, &c., *Op. cit.*, pp. 46 ff.; Funk, *Op. cit.*, pp. 9 ff.; Kirsopp Lake, *Op. cit.*, i, pp. 337 ff.

(*d*) *Pliny's Letter to Trajan*,[1] belonging to about the year A.D. 112, offers only indirect evidence for our purposes, and very little regarding the elements of liturgical worship; but that little is not without interest. The letter was written in reference to Christians in Bithynia.

(*e*) The *Ignatian Epistles*[2] belong to the years A.D. 110–117; they were written to various Christian communities in Asia Minor. Ignatius was condemned to be martyred in the amphitheatre at Rome, and during his journey from Antioch in Syria, of which he was bishop, to Rome, he passed through different places in which the Church had been founded—Ephesus, Magnesia, Tralles; while in Smyrna he wrote epistles to these communities, as well as to the Christians in Rome. Later, when he had reached Troas, he wrote further epistles to the churches in Philadelphia and Smyrna, also to Polycarp, bishop of Smyrna.

Although for our present purposes these epistles offer but little, they contain some indirect evidence which is of value; they must, therefore, be taken into consideration. As in the case of the *Epistle of Barnabas*, though not to the same extent, they contain some anti-Judaic passages (e. g. Magn. viii, ix, x; Philadelph. vi); on the other hand, in speaking of the Passion of Christ, Ignatius says that it was that 'He might set up an ensign for all ages through His Resurrection, for His saints and believers, whether among the Jews, or among the Gentiles, in one body of His church' (Smyrn. i. 2).

---

[1] Lightfoot, *Op. cit.*, Part II, vol. i, pp. 50 ff.

[2] Gebhardt, &c., *Op. cit.*, pp. 87 ff.; Funk, *Op. cit.*, pp. 81 ff.; Lightfoot, *Op. cit.*, Part II, vol. ii, sections i and ii; Kirsopp Lake, *Op. cit.*, i, pp. 172 ff.

(*f*) One of the most valuable documents for the present investigation is the *Didaché*,[1] or 'The Teaching of the Twelve Apostles'. It gives us direct and detailed evidence on the early liturgical worship of the Church. Its date is probably about the middle of the second century at the latest, though some writers place it at the end of the first century. The work is anonymous, and is addressed 'to the Gentiles'. Its place of origin is unknown. It consists of two quite independent parts, i–vi, and vii–xv; the last chapter, xvi, belonged originally to the first part, in all likelihood; only the second part comes into consideration here. Its use by early Church writers is evidence of the authority it enjoyed; and its importance, according to one whose knowledge of early Judaism makes his opinion especially valuable, lies above all in the fact that it has come down to us 'from the primitive age in which Christianity had but just separated itself from the parent stock of Judaism' (Taylor, *Op. cit.*, p. 118).

(*g*) The so-called *Second Epistle of Clement*[2] is included here as it gives one or two indications of Jewish influence which are worth noting. It belongs to the middle of the second century, and was probably

---

[1] Taylor, *The Teaching of the Twelve Apostles with illustrations from the Talmud* (1886); Rendel Harris, *The Teaching of the Apostles* (1887); Harnack, *Die Apostellehre und die jüdischen beiden Wege* (1886); see also his *Geschichte der altchristlichen Literatur*, pp. 86 ff. (1893); Funk, ' Die Didaché . . . ', in *Kirchengeschichtliche Abhandl. und Untersuchungen*, ii (1899); Seeberg, *Die beiden Wege und das Aposteldekret* (1905), and *Die Didaché des Judentums und der Urchristenheit* (1908); Kirsopp Lake, *Op. cit.*, i, pp. 308 ff.; J. Armitage Robinson, *Barnabas, Hermas, and the Didaché* (1920); Bigg and Maclean, *The Doctrine of the Twelve Apostles* (1922).

[2] Lightfoot, *Op. cit.*, Part I, vol. ii, pp. 211 ff.; Gebhardt, &c., *Op. cit.*, pp. 35 ff.; Funk, *Op. cit.*, pp. 69 ff.; Kirsopp Lake, *Op. cit.*, i, pp. 128 ff.

written from Rome. It is a sermon, not an epistle.

(*h*) To the same period belongs the *Epistle of Polycarp*[1] to the Philippians, written from Smyrna. It contains a few points of interest for our present investigation.

(*i*) Of first importance are some passages from *Justin Martyr's First Apology* and from his *Dialogue with Trypho*; from these we are able to gather some instructive details regarding the liturgical worship of the early Church. Justin was born about A.D. 100, and suffered martyrdom not later than the year 167.[2]

(*j*) Some interesting *data* are also to be gleaned from *Irenaeus'* work *Adversus Haereses*, written about A.D. 180. Irenaeus was born in Asia Minor, and became bishop of Lyons about A.D. 130; in his youth he was well acquainted with Polycarp.[3]

(*k*) *Clement of Alexandria*, born in the middle of the second century, gives some incidental references to liturgical worship in his *Stromateis*, in *Qui dives salvetur*, and in the *Paedagogus*; these works belong approximately to the end of the second century.[4]

---

[1] Lightfoot, *Op. cit.*, Part II, vol. ii, section ii, pp. 905 ff. ; Gebhardt, &c., *Op. cit.*, pp. 114 ff. ; Funk, *Op. cit.*, pp. 101 ff.; Kirsopp Lake, *Op. cit.*, i, pp. 282 ff.

[2] J. C. T. Otto, *Corpus Apologetarum Christianorum saeculi secundi*, I. ii (1877), Greek text of the Dialogue; Krüger, *Die Apologieen Justins des Märtyrers* (1896), and *Geschichte der altchristlichen Literatur*, pp. 65 ff. (1898); Harnack, *Judentum und Judenchristentum in Justins Dialog mit Trypho* (1913).

[3] Migne, *Patr. Gr.* vii, cols. 437 ff.; Harnack, *Lehrbuch der Dogmengeschichte*, i, pp. 550 ff. (1909); Hitchcock, *St. Irenaeus : Against the Heresies* (1916).

[4] For the *Stromateis*, see Migne, *PG* ix, and for the *Paedagogus*,

(*l*) The *Acts of John* is a Gnostic work belonging probably to about the middle of the second century, though some authorities place it half a century later. In spite of much heretical teaching (see, for example, its Docetism in chaps. xcvii ff.), it offers some important evidence for the early forms of Christian worship, especially in chaps. cvi–cx.[1]

(*m*) *The Epistle of the Apostles*. This is another apocryphal book, belonging, according to Schmidt, to about the year 160. We mention it here for completeness' sake, though there is only one passage from it to which we refer.[2]

These are the sources of evidence for the first two centuries.

II

(*a*) The third and fourth century documents offer some perplexing problems concerning which considerable diversity of opinion exists. These problems do not, it is true, affect very greatly the particular investigation with which we are concerned ; but we have, of course, done our best, by consulting the works of experts, to reach some definite conclusions ; and we feel convinced that those reached by Dom Connolly and put forth in his *The So-called Egyptian Church*

viii; for the *Qui dives salvetur*, Butterworth, *Clement of Alexandria*, pp. 270 ff., in Loeb's Classical Library (1919); mention may also be made of Barnard's English translation of *Qui dives salvetur* (1901).

[1] Bonnet, *Acta Apost. Apocr.* ii. 1 (1898); M. R. James, *The Apocryphal New Testament*, pp. 228 ff. (1924); an admirable account of the work is given by A. F. Findlay, *Byways in Early Christian Literature*, pp. 208 ff. (1923).

[2] M. R. James, *Op. cit.*, pp. 485 ff., where an English translation is given.

Order and Derived Documents ('Texts and Studies', vol. viii, no. 4, 1916) compel acceptance.[1] We therefore follow him. He shows that the *Egyptian Church Order*, belonging to the early third century, and which in its original Greek title was ascribed to Hippolytus, is the source of all the other Church Orders. It exists in four versions, the Ethiopic, Arabic, Coptic (Sahidic), and Latin; these four versions 'give us what is essentially one and the same document; and to treat the Ethiopic, Coptic, and Latin versions as in any sense separate and independent redactions of some earlier form of the document is to introduce an unnecessary element of confusion into a problem already sufficiently complex' (p. 4).

The Testament of our Lord is also derived from the *Egyptian Church Order*; but it is 'strongly marked by the individuality of its compiler'; it belongs approximately to the middle of the fourth century. To the latter half of this century belong the *Apostolic Constitutions*, viii. 3 ff.,[2] and the *Canons of Hippolytus*[3]; both are likewise derived from the *Egyptian Church Order*. The document called *Constitutiones per Hippolytum* is 'merely an excerpt from the "Apostolic Constitutions", bk. viii, made by a later hand' (Connolly, p. 6).

The following is a selection of the published editions of these documents and translations:

Hauler, *Didascaliae Apostolorum fragmenta veronensia latina* (1900).
Horner, *The Statutes of the Apostles* (1904).
Connolly, *The So-called Egyptian Church Order and Derived*

---

[1] See also Srawley's appreciative review in *JTS* xviii, pp. 229 ff. (1917).

[2] Chapters i–vi of this work are based on the third cent. *Didascalia*.

[3] Sections xix, xx, xxviii ff. are those which mainly concern us.

Documents (1916), Appendix B is a continuous text of the whole of the Egyptian Church Order, Hauler's Latin fragments being printed in their entirety, and the *lacunae* being filled in by an English translation from Horner's work mentioned above.

Funk, *Die apostolischen Konstitutionen* (1891).

Funk, *Didascalia et Constitutiones Apostolorum* (1905).

Turner, *A Primitive Edition of the Apostolic Constitutions*, *JTS* xiv. 53 ff. (1913).

Funk, *Das Testament unseres Herrn und die verwandten Schriften* (1901).

Cooper and Maclean, *The Testament of our Lord* (1902).

Achelis, *Die Canones Hippolyti* ('Texte und Untersuchungen' vi. 4 [1891]).

Riedel, *Die Kirchenrechtsquellen des Patriarchats Alexandrien*, pp. 200 ff. (1900).

See also, Brightman, *Liturgies Eastern and Western* (1896).

Wordsworth, *The Ministry of Grace* (1901).

Maclean, *The Ancient Church Orders* (1910).

(*b*) A work very different from the foregoing, and in which one would not at first expect to find much information for present purposes, is the apocryphal *Acts of Thomas*. It is, however, both important and interesting. The book is 'a product of the Syriac-speaking Church and reflects the spirit and ideals which prevailed in Eastern Christianity for a considerable period both before and after its appearance';[1] this was in all probability in the second quarter of the third century. It has been preserved in its entirety. The author 'belonged to that portion of the Eastern Church which had its main centre in Edessa', and 'in

---

[1] Findlay, *Op. cit.*, pp. 273 ff. The Greek text is published by Bonnet, *Actes de Saint Thomas, apôtre* (1907); an English translation is published by James, *Op. cit.*, pp. 365 ff. ; the Syriac text is given in W. Wright's *Apocryphal Acts of the Apostles*, vol. i, pp. 172 ff., English translation, vol. ii, pp. 46 ff. (1871); Bedjan, *Sharbē dsohᵃdhē wadqaddīshē* (Acta Martyrum et Sanctorum) iii, pp. 1–175 (1892).

spite of ecclesiastical condemnation from the fourth century onwards, the book continued to be read in orthodox circles throughout the Church . . . ; in respect of doctrine there is almost nothing in it to give offence to catholic sentiment '. The relevant chapters for our purpose are xxix, xlix, l, cxxxiii, clviii.

(*c*) A few details are also to be gained from one or two of the writings of *Origen* [1] and *Tertullian* [2] to which reference will be made below. Origen was a younger contemporary of Clement of Alexandria ; Tertullian lived during the first half of the third century. Slightly later is *Cyprian* (he was martyred in 258) ; in chap. xxxi of his *De Orat. Dom.* and in his sixty-third letter he gives some liturgical *data* of importance. [3]

(*d*) For the fourth century we have in Cyril of Jerusalem's *Catechesis Mystagogica*, v some important liturgical *data* ; [4] but as, unfortunately, he does not give the text of the more developed Liturgy of this century, his evidence is not so useful for our particular purpose as for the general history of the Liturgy. The date of his *Catechesis* is the middle of this century.

(*e*) To this period belongs also the *Liturgy of Sarapion*, discovered in the Laura monastery on Mount Athos. For the Greek text see Brightman in *JTS*, i, pp. 88 ff., 247 ff. ; an English translation

---

[1] The details are gathered mainly from his homilies on the books of the Bible, in Migne, *PG* xi, xii, xiii ; for *Contra Cels.*, Migne, xi.

[2] For the *Apol.* and *De cult. fem.*, Migne, i ; for *De Anim.*, *De Orat.*, and *De Spectac.*, Reiffenscheid and Wissowa in *Corp. Script. Eccl. Lat.*, xx.

[3] De Romestin in *St. Cyril on the Mysteries*, pp. 104 ff. (1887).

[4] The Greek text is given by Woolley, *Op. cit.*, pp. 178 ff. ; De Romestin, *Op. cit.*, pp. 34 ff.

will be found in Wordsworth's *Bishop Sarapion's Prayer-Book* (1910).   This Liturgy was first published by Wobbermin in *Altchristliche liturgische Stücke...*, pp. 4 ff. (1899).[1]   The Anaphora is given in §§ 1 ff., the pro-anaphoral prayers in §§ 19 ff.

Other authorities are incidentally referred to in the following pages ; the editions used will be indicated in foot-notes.

[1] In Gebhardt und Harnack's *Texte und Untersuchungen zur Geschichte der altchristlichen Literatur* (Neue Folge, II, Heft 3 *b*).

V

THE INFLUENCE OF THE JEWISH LITURGY ON EARLY FORMS OF CHRISTIAN WORSHIP

In Chapter II we examined those elements of the Jewish Liturgy which there is every reason to believe were pre-Christian in their original form. How long these elements remained unconnected with the specifically Christian eucharistic service it is impossible to say with certainty. But at an early period, as the evidence indicates, some parts of the synagogal liturgy were adopted by the Church as an introductory service to the Eucharist proper. Not only so; but, as we hope to be able to show, some elements of the Jewish Liturgy were incorporated in the eucharistic service itself, and have, in one form or another, remained there to the present day.

The sections in this chapter, dealing with the various elements in the worship of the early Church, will correspond, as far as possible, with the sections of Chapter II.

I. THE READING OF SCRIPTURE AND THE EXPOSITION.

As among the Jews, so among the Jewish and Gentile Christians, knowledge of the Scriptures was gained, in the main, by hearing them read during the public services. We say that this was the case *in the main*, but it was not the exclusive means of studying the Bible, for we have evidence that copies of individual books were, perhaps not infrequently, in private possession. Though not our immediate concern, it will be of interest if we point briefly to some of the evidence of the existence of Scripture rolls in private possession; and here, as in other directions, Jewish practice was followed by the early Christians.

First in reference to the Jews: from 1 Macc. i. 56, 57 it is clear that rolls of the Law were to be found in private houses, for possessors of such were, according to the royal decree, to be put to death. Again, reference to the purchase of books of the Scriptures by individuals is made in the Mishnah, *Megilla* iii. 1. In *Jebamoth* xvi. 7 it is told of how the son of a Levite fell ill while on a journey, and was brought to an inn, where he died; among his belongings a roll of the Law was found. Another example of a book of the Bible being in private possession is seen in Acts viii. 28, where it is told of the Ethiopian eunuch that he was 'sitting in his chariot and was reading the prophet Isaiah'. Nevertheless, it cannot be doubted that this was exceptional; for, in the first place, the number of those able to read was limited, and this in spite of the existence of many a *Beth ha-sepher*, i.e. 'House of the book', where boys were taught the elements of the Law; for, since in these institutions the main thing was the *teaching* of the Law, it does not necessarily follow that the pupils were taught to read. Again, copies of scriptural books were limited, for the art of writing was even more restricted than that of reading. And though the cost of rolls was comparatively moderate, there were but few who could afford to buy them.[1]

[1] On the whole subject much valuable information is to be gained

That copies of the Scriptures in private houses is not generally to be looked for, however, may be gathered from Col. iii. 16: 'Let the word of Christ dwell in you richly in all wisdom; teaching and admonishing one another with psalms and hymns and spiritual songs' (cp. Eph. v. 19); no mention is here made of the reading of Scripture; this must be due to the fact that copies of them were not, as a rule, available in the home. An exception to this occurs in 2 Tim. iii. 15, 'from a babe thou hast known the sacred writings', for this evidently refers to home reading of the Scriptures. On the other hand, 1 Tim. iv. 13, 'Till I come give heed to reading (πρόσεχε τῇ ἀναγνώσει), to exhortation, to teaching', is said in reference to public worship.[1]

In Acts xvii. 11 reference is made to the Synagogue of the Jews of Berœa who examined the Scriptures daily 'whether these things were so'. This suggests that in the Synagogues of the Dispersion access could be had to the rolls of Scripture (Greek) at any time, just as, presumably, was the case in the Synagogues of Palestine (cp. Lk. ii. 46, 47; Jn. v. 39).

While, then, there were exceptions to the general rule, there can be no doubt that the reading and explanation of the Scriptures during public worship in the Synagogue was the chief way whereby the knowledge of them was disseminated; hence the supreme importance of the custom.

from Birt, *Das antike Buchwesen* (1882); Blau, *Studien zum althebräischen Buchwesen* (1902); Harnack, *Privater Gebrauch der heiligen Schriften in der alten Kirche* (1912).

[1] So far as Palestinian Jews were concerned it will be realized that the bulk of the people would not have been able to understand their Scriptures, since they were written in Hebrew, even if they possessed copies.

This custom was followed when Jewish Christians met together for worship. Col. iv. 16 shows the beginning of the reading of specifically Christian writings, in addition to the Old Testament Scriptures, during the public worship of the Church: 'And when this epistle hath been read among you, cause that it be read also in the church of the Laodiceans; and that ye also read the epistle from Laodicea.' For the present, of course, no such epistles would be regarded as Scripture. Up to the second half of the second century A. D. the Church understood by 'the Scriptures' the books of the Old Testament.

We come now to examine the evidence of early Christian writers.

(1) Nowhere in 1 *Clement* is there any reference to the reading of Scripture as a part of the liturgical service. Not that this need cause surprise, for an intimate knowledge of the Scriptures is taken for granted throughout the epistle, and, as we have seen, this would have been gained mainly through hearing them read and expounded during public service. A few illustrations from 1 *Clement* will be instructive as showing that familiarity with the Scriptures among his readers is taken for granted by the writer.

This is seen again and again in the first twelve chapters, for example, when he appeals to the Scriptures in confirmation of what he is urging. ' Let us do that which is written', he says (xiii. 1), and then makes various quotations from the Old Testament. Moreover, the knowledge of the divisions of the Old Testament Canon is taken for granted; thus, in xxviii. 3 'the Writing'[1] ($\tau\grave{o}$ $\gamma\rho\alpha\phi\epsilon\hat{\iota}o\nu$ = $\dot{\alpha}\gamma\iota\acute{o}\gamma\rho\alpha\phi\alpha$) is spoken of, and

---

[1] The name corresponds with the title of the third division of the Hebrew Canon (*Kethubim*).

a quotation from the Psalms follows; in xliii. 1 the term 'the holy books' is applied to the Pentateuch (the Law), while by 'the other prophets' (i.e. besides Moses) the prophetical books are obviously meant. An interesting point is raised by the words in xlv. 2, 'Ye have pored over the holy Scriptures' (ἐνκεκύφατε εἰς τὰς ἱερὰς γραφάς); this may conceivably refer to the private use of the Scriptures; or it may allude to the study of the Scriptures in some place of worship where they were kept, as in the case of the Jews' Synagogue in Berœa, for the faithful to make use of when they wished; or it may refer to the earnest listening to the exposition after the reading of Scripture during the liturgical service. There is a similar reference in lxii. 3: '. . . we knew quite well that we were writing to faithful and elect men who had pored over the oracles of the teaching of God'; and again in liii. 1: 'Ye have a good understanding of the Holy Scriptures, beloved, and have pored over the oracles of God.' [1]

The reference to St. Paul's first epistle to the Corinthians in lxvii is interesting; for while this had evidently been treasured by the Church there, it does not appear from Clement's words to be regarded as Scripture yet; he says: 'Take up the epistle of the blessed Paul the Apostle'; the context shows he is referring to 1 Corinthians.[1]

The evidence of Clement is to the effect that the Old Testament Scriptures were very well known to his hearers; it is reasonable to suppose that this was, in the case of most, due to their being read and expounded to the assembled congregation during

---

[1] The words of Christ are often quoted, but it does not appear that the Gospels were yet spoken of as Scripture.

divine service. There is, on the other hand, no direct evidence in this source of Scripture reading being part of the liturgical service.

(2) The same must be said of the *Epistle of Barnabas*; but it is possible that in two passages we may discern indirect references to the reading of the Scriptures during the services. In xxi. 1 it is said : ' It is good, therefore, for him who has learned the ordinances of the Lord, as many as have been written (ὅσα γέγραπται), to walk in them '; and again in verse 6 : ' Be taught of God, seeking out (ἐκζητοῦντες) what the Lord requires of you.'

(3) With regard to *Ignatius* we can only repeat what was said about Clement on the subject; an intimate knowledge of the Scriptures among his various readers is taken for granted, and this knowledge was presumably gained, in the main, from hearing them read and explained at divine worship. A definite reference to *preaching* occurs in his epistle to Polycarp v. 1 : 'Flee from the evil arts [i.e. of false teachers] but rather preach against them (μᾶλλον δὲ περὶ τούτων ὁμιλίαν ποιοῦ).'

(4) That there is no mention of Scripture reading or the Sermon in the account of Sunday worship in the *Didaché* is because the introductory part of the service in which these occurred is not spoken of; it is only the Eucharist proper with which the writer deals. Nevertheless, it is possible that Scripture reading is alluded to in xvi. 2, where it says : ' But gather yourselves together frequently (πυκνῶς δὲ συναχθήσεσθε) seeking the things that are profitable for your souls.'

(5) The so-called *Second Epistle of Clement* is perhaps itself a sermon; at any rate, according to xix. 1,

it is an exhortation 'to give heed to the things that are written' (τοῖς γεγραμμένοις, i.e. the Scriptures) ; and it continues : 'that ye may both save yourselves and him who is the reader among you' (τὸν ἀναγινώσκοντα ἐν ὑμῖν). Whether this points to a definite order of readers may be doubted (see the next section), but the title 'reader' witnesses of course to the reading of Scripture as a fixed element in the Liturgy.

(6) *Justin Martyr* is the first to give us really clear and definite evidence of the reading of Scripture and the Sermon or homily following it as an integral part of divine worship. In the first *Apology* (i. 67) he says : Συνέλευσις γίνεται καὶ τὰ ἀπομνημονεύματα τῶν ἀποστόλων ἢ τὰ συγγράμματα τῶν προφητῶν ἀναγινώσκεται, μέχρις ἐγχωρεῖ· εἶτα, παυσαμένου τοῦ ἀναγινώσκοντος, ὁ προεστὼς διὰ λόγου τὴν νουθεσίαν καὶ πρόκλησιν τῆς τῶν καλῶν τούτων μιμήσεως ποιεῖται. There was clearly freedom of choice here regarding what was read ; and the phrase 'as far as time permitted' (μέχρις ἐγχωρεῖ) shows that the passages were not fixed. This reflects the usage of the Jewish Church at the beginning of the Christian era ; there were no fixed lessons. The technical terms *Parashah,* the 'section', or lesson from the Law, and *Haftarah,* the 'conclusion', or lesson from the Prophets which concluded the Scripture reading, were unknown at that time (cp. Mishnah, *Megilla* iv. 9, and see Zunz, *Op. cit.,* p. 3). It is evident that, in Christian as well as in Jewish worship, whatever passages were read, the choice was left to the reader, and the length of them was decided by him. The reader was, in all probability, not yet an official ; in this, as in the matter of Scripture reading and the homily which followed, the usage of the Jewish Church is likely to have been that of the early Christian Church ; any one could be called from among

the assembled worshippers to read, even a boy under twelve years might do so.[1]

Twice in the *Dialogue* Justin speaks of the reading of Scripture and the Sermon as part of liturgical worship : . . . ἀπό τε τῶν γραφῶν καὶ τῶν πραγμάτων τάς τε ἀποδείξεις καὶ τὰς ὁμιλίας ποιοῦμαι (xxviii) ; and in lxxxv : . . . τὸν ἀπὸ τῶν γραφῶν τῶν προφητικῶν ὁμιλίας ποιούμενον. It is doubtless in the light of these definite statements that the vague allusions to the subject in earlier Christian writings must be read.

(7) One or two references to other early Christian writers may be given, though it is doubtless, as in the case of Justin, long established use of which they speak. In the following passage from *Irenaeus* there may be the thought of Scripture reading and exposition during divine service ; speaking of the faithful believer he says : . . . *si et scripturas diligenter legerit apud eos qui in ecclesia sunt presbyteri, apud quos est apostolica doctrina.*[2]

Clement of Alexandria speaks of Scripture reading and what he calls 'true inquiry', i.e. the exposition.[3]

Origen has a number of references to the subject ;

[1] Mishnah, *Meg.* iv. 5, 6. On Scripture reading and the homily in the Synagogue at the beginning of the Christian era, Philo says : Τί οὖν ἐποίησε [i. e. ὁ νομοθέτης] ταῖς ἑβδόμαις ταύταις ἡμέραις ; Αὐτοὺς εἰς ταὐτὸν ἠξίου συνάγεσθαι, καὶ καθεζομένους μετ' ἀλλήλων σὺν αἰδοῖ καὶ κόσμῳ τῶν νόμων ἀκροᾶσθαι τοῦ μηδένα ἀγνοῆσαι χάριν. Καὶ δῆτα συνέρχονται μὲν ἀεί, καὶ συνεδρεύουσι μετ' ἀλλήλων· ἃ μὲν πολλοὶ σιωπῇ, πλὴν εἴ τι προσεπιφημίσαι τοῖς ἀναγινωσκομένοις νομίζεται· τῶν ἱερέων δέ τις ὁ παρὼν ἢ τῶν γερόντων εἰς ἀναγινώσκει τοὺς ἱεροὺς νόμους αὐτοῖς, καὶ καθ' ἕκαστον ἐξηγεῖται μέχρι σχεδὸν δείλης ὀψίας (Mangey ii. 630). On the title of προεστώς, who, according to Justin, gives the exhortation, see Deissmann, *Licht vom Orient*, pp. 139–43 (1908).

[2] iv. 33. 1, quoted by Harnack, *Privater Gebrauch* . . ., p. 37.

[3] *Stromateis* vi. 14 (Migne, *PG* ix, col. 338).

in *Contra Cels.* iii. 50 he says : καὶ δι' ἀναγνωσμάτων καὶ διὰ τῶν εἰς αὐτὰ διηγήσεων προτρέποντες μὲν ἐπὶ τὴν εἰς τὸν Θεὸν τῶν ὅλων εὐσέβειαν καὶ τὰς συνθρόνους ταύτῃ ἀρετάς, ἀποτρέποντες δὲ . . . ;[1] see also *In Exod. hom.* xiii. 1,[2] *In Luc. hom.*[3]

Tertullian, in speaking of the Sunday morning service, says, . . . *prout Scripturae leguntur aut psalmi canuntur aut allocutiones proferuntur aut petitiones delegantur* (*De Anima* ix) ; and his phrase *Administratio Dei verbi* (*De cult. fem.* ii. 11)[4] evidently refers to the preparatory portion of the Liturgy during which the Scriptures were read and explained (cp. Acts vi. 4, ἡ διακονία τοῦ λόγου).

Cyril of Jerusalem speaks of the twenty-two books of the Divine Scriptures ἃς καὶ ἐν Ἐκκλησίᾳ μετὰ παρρησίας ἀναγινώσκομεν (*Cat.* iv. 35).

Plenty of further evidence could be given ; it will suffice to give a few references to the Church Orders.

In Bk. ii of the *Apost. Const.* there is an enumeration of the sacred books from which the lessons are to be read. After the Gospel has been read it is directed that the priests, the deacons, and the people shall stand in silence, 'for it is written, "Be silent and Hear, O Israel" . . .'[5] It is worth mentioning, in passing, that the words, 'Hear, O Israel', in connexion with the reading of the Law in the Synagogue service occurs in the tractate *Sopherim* xiv, which contains so much ancient traditional material. It is quite possible that we have here an echo of synagogue usage.

In Bk. viii of the *Apost. Const.* (the 'Clementine' Liturgy) there is a reference to the reading of the

---

[1] Migne, *PG* xi, col. 986.
[2] *Ibid.*, xii, col. 388.
[3] *Ibid.*, xiii, col. 1819.
[4] *Ibid.*, i, col. 1329.
[5] Brightman, *Op. cit.*, p. 29.

Law, the Prophets, the Epistles and Acts, and the Gospel.[1]

In the twenty-seventh of the *Canons of Hippolytus* it is laid down that every Christian should study the Scriptures daily, having heard them read during divine service.

In view, then, of what we have seen to have been the case regarding the reading of the Scriptures in the Synagogue service, with the exposition which followed, in pre-Christian times, there can be no question about the fact that in this the Church followed the guidance of the Synagogue.

A final point may be mentioned as being not without interest. In the *Egyptian Church Order* there is a section regarding instruction in the Holy Scriptures from which we quote the following :

' Concerning the times at which it is seemly to pray, and to hear instruction . . . All believing men and women, having risen at dawn, before they do any work, should wash their hands and pray to God ; and then turn to their works ; and if they tell them where is the word of instruction, every one shall choose to go thither to the place of instruction . . . And it shall be reckoned great loss to him who fears God if he goes not to where is the place of instruction, and especially for him who can read. And if there is an instructor he shall not defer (from going) to the church and the place where is the instruction . . . and if there is a day on which there is no instruction, every one shall stay in his house and shall take the holy Scripture and read it as well as he can, for it is good' (*Stat.* 48).[2]

The ' place of instruction ' in this passage is not synonymous with the church, for the possibility is contemplated of there being no instruction on occasion,

---

[1] Brightman, p. 3.

[2] Dom Connolly, *Op. cit.*, pp. 191 ff. ; cp. *Apost. Const.* i. 5.

whereas, according to the *Apost. Const.* ii. 59, there was a daily morning and evening service in the Lord's House ; this, too, being founded on the pattern of the Synagogue. The 'place of instruction' must, we think, be a Christian adaptation of the *Beth ha-Midrash*, 'House of instruction'. This was an ancient institution among the Jews ; as early as about 180 B.C. it was already well known, according to the *Wisdom of Ben-Sira* li. 23 ff. The *Beth ha-Midrash* was often attached to the Synagogue for convenience' sake, but it was quite distinct from this. The same would appear to have been the case in the early Church, which would account for the somewhat ambiguous terms in the *Egyptian Church Order* ; for in one passage the 'church' and the 'place of instruction' seem to be identified.

This was, therefore, another way whereby a knowledge of the Scriptures was gained; nevertheless, it was the reading of them and the exposition in the public worship which was the chief means for this, because attendance at a 'place of instruction' would be confined, generally speaking, to those who had leisure, and not to the mass who had to attend to their daily work.

II. The Influence of the Shema'.

The supreme importance of the *Shema'* in the Jewish Church, and its position in the Jewish Liturgy as the nearest approach to a creed, has been pointed out. The doctrine of the unity of God which it expressed was the foundation-stone of Judaism. The first Jewish Christians were accustomed to recite the *Shema'* twice daily, and therefore it cannot be doubted that they were strongly influenced by its teaching. In the Synagogues of the Dispersion (i. e. in pagan surroundings) which welcomed the presence of Gentile converts its influence would have been specially salutary.

But the question arises as to whether any marks of this influence can be discerned in the early Church; and, above all, whether the early Christian communities were influenced in their doctrine of God by the *Shema'*. There are some facts which may or may not point to such influence; but in any case they are worth drawing attention to in this connexion.

We may begin by pointing to the well-known fact that in the narrative portions of the earliest Gospel (St. Mark) Christ is scarcely ever spoken of as 'Lord', which seems to point to a certain hesitation in speaking of Him as God. In writing about the *Gospel of the Nazarenes*, Findlay remarks that 'the name "the Lord" applied to Jesus in descriptive narrative—a usage that is very rare in Matthew and Mark and comparatively frequent in Luke and John—seems to have been common in the Nazarene Gospel. In this respect it is similar to the Gospel of Peter. It is a mark of a relatively late date.'[1] But further, in reading such an early document as 1 *Clement* one cannot fail to gain the impression that a certain subordination, as compared with the Father, is assigned to Christ; see, for example, chap. xxxvi. It is true that the title 'Lord' is applied to Christ about a dozen times, but far more frequently He is spoken of without this epithet being applied to Him; and He is never spoken of as God. The title 'Master' is often used, but always in reference to God the Father.

[1] *Byways in Early Christian Literature*, p. 71 (1923).

On the other hand, Ignatius in all his epistles, and Polycarp in his epistle to the Philippians, as well as Barnabas, teach the full doctrine of the dual nature of Christ. But then again, when one turns to the *Didaché* one becomes aware that there is to some extent a reticence in regard to Christ's divinity. Speaking generally, though there are exceptions (e.g. *Ignat. to Polycarp* viii. 2 ; *Polycarp to the Phil.* xii. 2), the Apostolic Fathers do not speak of Christ directly as God. Then, once more, it is a noticeable fact that in our earliest liturgical records prayer is never addressed to Christ, but only to God the Father.[1] Origen says that prayer must be made ' in the Name of Jesus', but not directly addressed to Him (*De Orat.* xv) ; see also Augustine, *Confessions*, xi. 2, 22, where one sees that the tradition of primitive Christianity still holds sway. Whatever it may have been that gave birth to the tradition—and we believe that the *Shema'* was not without its influence in forming it—it evidently constituted a danger to early Christianity, to which the words of the middle second-century document known as 2 *Clement* bear witness ; this opens with the words : ' Brethren, we must think of Jesus Christ as of God, as of " the Judge of the living and the dead " ; and we must not think little of our salvation ; for if we think little of Him we also hope to obtain but little. . . .' It is evident that the writer must here have had in mind those who conceived inadequately of the nature of Christ.

From the earliest ages of Christianity two tendencies are to be discerned regarding the Person of Christ, each of which respectively laid special emphasis on His human and divine nature, with a view, in either case,

---

[1] See further on this Von der Goltz, *Gebet in der ältesten Christenheit*, p. 128 (1901); Bousset, *Kyrios Jesus*, pp. 102, 285 (1903).

of insisting upon the doctrine of the unity of God ; and the *development* of these tendencies began early. On the one hand, insistence upon Christ's humanity was a safeguard against there being any idea of more than one God ; and, on the other, insistence on His divinity by identifying Him with the Father likewise emphasized the doctrine of the unity of God. The latter opened the door to Docetism, which soon began to manifest itself ; the former ultimately issued in Arianism. Against those who held docetic views Ignatius, for example, writes : ' For what does any one profit me if he praise me, but blaspheme my Lord, and do not confess that He was clothed in flesh ? ' (*Smyrn.* v. 2) ; and against those who denied the divinity of Christ such words as those quoted above from 2 *Clement* are directed. But the point which we wish to emphasize is that what lay behind the ideas combated was the desire to uphold the doctrine of the unity of God, and that all this was, ultimately, due to the influence of the *Shema'*.

It was a little later, in the second half of the second century, that the literature arose which so fully illustrates the difficulty felt by many of believing in Christ while holding the doctrine of the unity of God, together with the teaching put forth for solving the difficulty.

With the history of the opposition offered to the doctrine of the Holy Trinity by those who claimed to champion monotheism we cannot deal here as it would take us too far from our present purpose.[1]

When, however, we remember how deeply rooted and venerated the *Shema'* and its teaching were among the Jews, and therefore among the Jewish Christians,

---

[1] A good *résumé* is given in M. Friedländer, *Synagoge und Kirche in ihren Anfängen,* pp. 226 ff. (1908).

it is difficult to resist the conclusion that the controversies of the Church during the earliest Christian
centuries regarding the doctrine of God must be
ultimately traced back to its influence.

III. PRAYER.

The influence of the Jewish Liturgy on the early
Church and its forms of worship is nowhere so clearly
to be discerned as in the prayers which have been
preserved in early Christian literature and in the
earliest forms of the Christian Liturgy.   Nobody, in
reading the pre-Christian forms of prayer in the Jewish
Liturgy and the prayers of the early Church, can fail
to notice the similarity of atmosphere of each, or to
recognize that both proceed from the same mould.
Even when one perceives, as often happens, variety in
the later form, the *genus* is unmistakable.

Before coming to a detailed comparison of some of
the prayers it will be well to offer some general
remarks on the subject so far as the early Church
is concerned, for this will show that we are moving
here in the same spiritual atmosphere as that of the
Synagogue.

The rule of the three hours of prayer of the daily
Synagogue worship was observed by the first Christians
(the third hour, Acts ii. 15 ; the sixth hour, Acts x. 9 ;
and the ninth hour, Acts iii. 1).[1]   In the Synagogue
the *Shemôneh 'Esreh* (or part of it, see above, p. 54)
was said at each of these three services.   In the same
way the Lord's Prayer was said thrice daily, according
to the *Didaché* (viii. 3).[2]   While it is evident, as we

---

[1] Tertullian (*De Jejun.* x) says this was based on apostolic practice.

[2] Later the hours of prayer were increased to five: at cock-crow,

shall see from the extracts to be given below, that fixed forms of prayer were used in the early Church, *extempore* prayer also played an important part. It is mentioned in the *Didaché* (ch. x, to which we refer below) and Tertullian speaks of this in his *Apol.* xxx. 39 : *Sine monitore, quia de pectore oramus, ut quisque de proprio ingenio posset.* Herein likewise the Church followed the synagogal pattern.

The marks which we saw to be characteristic of the Synagogue prayers are to be found in the prayers of the early Church. In the illustrations, which we shall give presently this will be seen : Praise and thanksgiving, especially for the power of God as seen in the Creation,[1] for His guardianship, for deliverance from evil, and for spiritual enlightenment, concluding with confession and prayer for forgiveness ; the petitions are less prominent, as in the Jewish prayers ; there is also the sense of corporateness which finds expression ; and, of course, there is intercessory prayer, one form of which is prayer for rulers ; the concluding doxology is likewise a necessary element of the prayers ; with the Amen we shall deal later. The historical reminiscences which occur in many of the Jewish prayers are often taken over by the Church and adapted in a Christian sense.

before retiring to rest, and the three mentioned above (cp. Origen, *De Orat.* xii ; Tertullian, *De Orat.* xxv ; Cyprian, *De Orat.* xxxiv). In the *Egyptian Church Order* the *reasons* for praying at the third, sixth, and ninth hours are given ; prayer at midnight is also enjoined (see Connolly, *Op. cit.*, p. 192).

[1] Cp. Rev. iv. 8 ff., where the heavenly worship is described, and honour and thanks are given to God for His power and for His act of creation ; this reflects the worship on earth. Origen (*De Orat.* xxxiii) says that praise and thanksgiving are the two primary τόποι of prayer.

To come now to some illustrations:

(*a*) We have seen, in dealing with prayer in the Jewish Church, that the *Shemôneh 'Esreh*, as the prayer *par excellence* of the Liturgy, occupies the central place. This must, therefore, be the first prayer to be compared with some of the early prayers of the Church.

Owing to the important place which the *Shemôneh 'Esreh* had in the worship of the Synagogue there may be some justification for believing that it was included in 'the prayers' spoken of in Acts ii. 42. It is also conceivable that this prayer was in Christ's mind in uttering the words: 'And when ye pray, ye shall not be as the hypocrites: for they love to stand and pray in the synagogues and in the corners of the streets, that they may be seen of men' (Matt. vi. 5; cp. Mk. xi. 25). This prayer, as we have seen, was said standing; and its being said elsewhere than in the Synagogue would be nothing out of the common (see, for example, Mishnah, *Ber*. iv. 2 ff.). Christ's words, however, were not spoken against the prayer itself, but against the wrong spirit in reciting it. The influence it had on early Church worship will be seen by comparing with it the long liturgical prayer in 1 *Clem*. lix. 3–lxi. 3.

1 *Clem.*	*Shem. 'Es.*
lix. 3. (Grant us) to hope in Thy Name, the first source of all creation; open the eyes of our heart to know Thee, that Thou alone art the Highest among the highest, and remainest Holy among the holy ones.	*Bened.* iii. Thou art holy, and holy is Thy Name; and holy ones praise Thee every day. Blessed art Thou, O Lord, the Holy God.

The central thoughts in each of these passages, which are clearly parallel, are the holiness of God, and the praise accorded to Him by the highest, i. e. the holy ones, by which are meant, of course, the angels.

Again:

Thou dost humble the pride of the haughty, that destroyest the imaginings of the nations, that settest on high the humble, that abasest the lofty, that makest rich and makest poor, that killest and makest alive, the only finder of spirits and God of all flesh; that lookest on the abysses, the discerner of the works of men, the helper of those in danger, the Saviour of them that despair, the Creator and Guardian (ἐπίσκοπον) of every spirit;
. . .

lix. 4. We beseech Thee, Master (δέσποτα), to be our help and succour. Save those of us who are in affliction, have mercy on the lowly, raise the fallen, manifest Thyself to the needy, heal the sick, turn those that are gone astray of Thy people; feed the hungry, ransom those who are bound, raise up the weak, comfort the fainthearted . . .

Bened. ii. Thou art mighty for ever, O Lord, O Thou that quickenest the dead, Thou art mighty to save . . .

Thou sustainest the living with mercy, that quickenest the dead; that dost support the fallen with great mercies, that healest the sick, that loosest the bound, that preservest alive (מְקַיֵּם) with them that sleep in the dust. Who is like unto Thee, Master (בַּעַל) of mighty acts; and who resembleth Thee, O King, that killest and makest alive, that causest salvation to spring forth?

One cannot read these two extracts without discerning the influence of the *Shemôneh 'Esreh* on the Christian liturgical prayer. The latter is somewhat expanded, but the thoughts and general content are the same. Very striking is the phrase ' Guardian of every spirit' when compared with the corresponding words of the Synagogue prayer, 'That preservest alive them that sleep in the dust', witnessing as it does to a higher spiritual conception. The use of the word ἐπίσκοπος in this connexion is interesting; Lightfoot compares Job x. 12 and 1 Pet. ii. 25.

The *Shemôneh 'Esreh* has, through the medium of this prayer in 1 *Clement* (and it was probably not the only medium), influenced the early liturgies of the Church; for, as Lightfoot says, ' it is impossible not to be struck with the resemblances in this passage to portions of the earliest known liturgies. Not only is there a general coincidence of the objects of the several petitions, but it has also individual phrases, and in one instance a whole cluster of petitions, in common with one or other of these.'[1] The references to these are given in his notes on the text.

Next, we may see how prayer for spiritual enlightenment, which finds expression in some of the early Christian documents, follows the synagogal prayers. The fourth Benediction of the *Shemôneh 'Esreh* has this petition :

Thou dost favourably grant knowledge unto men,
And dost teach discernment unto men ;
Grant us from Thee knowledge and understanding and
    discernment.
Blessed art Thou who dost graciously grant knowledge.

[1] *Apostolic Fathers*, Part i, St. Clement of Rome, vol. i, pp. 384 ff. (1890).

In a different form, but the same in essence, a similar petition occurs in the *'Ahabah* prayer (see p. 48, above) :

> O our Father, our King, for our fathers' sake, who trusted in Thee, and whom Thou didst teach the statutes of life, be gracious unto us too, and teach us. Enlighten our eyes in Thy Law, and let our hearts cleave unto Thy commandments, and unite our hearts to love and fear Thy Name ; that we may never be put to confusion.

With these we may compare the following extract from a prayer in the *Liturgy of Sarapion* :

> '. . . Grant us knowledge and faith and piety and sanctification. Take away every passion, every lust, every sin from this people ; make them all to be pure. . . . Give us holy understanding and perfect usefulness. Grant that we may seek Thee and love Thee. Grant that we may search Thy divine words and study them. Stretch out Thine hand unto us, O Master, and raise us up. Raise us up, O God of mercies, that we may look upwards ; open our eyes ; grant us boldness. . . .' [1]

As in other cases, the Christian prayer is fuller and more elaborate ; but then it must be remembered that the forms in which these early prayers have come down to us are developed from simpler forms ; the process was a natural one, and indeed inevitable ; it is to be paralleled with what happened, as we have seen, in the case of the synagogal prayers. But it is in the spirit and content of the Christian forms of prayer that we must discern Jewish influence.

Our next illustration is from the *Didaché* which betrays the influence of another of the *Shemôneh 'Esreh* Benedictions. In *Did.* ix. 9 there is recorded

---

[1] Wobbermin, *Altchristliche liturgische Stücke*, p. 18.

the offering of a prayer which follows immediately after the consecration of the eucharistic elements.[1] That this prayer is reminiscent of the tenth Benediction of the *Shemôneh 'Esreh* will be seen by comparing the two :

Didaché.	*Shem. 'Es. (Bened.* x.)
As this broken bread was scattered upon the mountains, but was brought together and became one, so let Thy Church be gathered together from the ends of the earth into Thy Kingdom ; for Thine is the glory and the power through Jesus Christ for ever.	Sound the great horn (תְּקַע בְּשׁוֹפָר) for our freedom ; and lift up the ensign (וְשָׂא נֵס) to gather our exiles, and gather us together from the four corners of the earth. Blessed art Thou, O Lord, that gatherest the outcasts of Israel.

This reads like a Christian adaptation of the Jewish Benediction. Behind both lies, in all probability, Isa. xviii. 3 : 'All the inhabitants of the world, and ye dwellers on the earth, when an ensign is lifted up (כִּנְשֹׂא־נֵס) on the mountains, see ye ; and when the trumpet is blown (וְכִתְקֹעַ שׁוֹפָר), hear ye.'

In the prayer which follows the thanksgiving (*Did.* x. 5, 6) there is again the thought of gathering the Church together, and a phrase very similar to that of

---

[1] We assume that the reference in this passage is to the Eucharist, both because it is directly asserted in verse 1, and because the expression 'broken bread' seems to imply it ; and see further below. We are aware, however, that some writers hold that it is the *Agapé* which is here described, e. g. Bigg, *The Doctrine of the Twelve Apostles*, pp. 24 f. (2nd ed. with a new Introduction and revised notes by A. J. Maclean, 1922); but we do not find his arguments convincing.

the Benediction occurs : ' Gather it together . . . from the four winds.' And at the conclusion comes the purely Jewish sentence : ' Hosannah to the God of David.'

But a Thanksgiving (x. 2–4) precedes this prayer ; it is said ' after ye have been filled '. Presumably the reference here is to the *Agapé*.[1] In any case, though it is Christian in character, its Jewish form is unmistakable : ' We give thanks to Thee, O Holy Father, for Thy holy Name which Thou didst make to tabernacle in our hearts, and for the knowledge and faith and immortality which Thou didst make known to us.' This is Jewish ; it is only the addition of the words, ' through Thy Servant Jesus ', which give it a Christian character. Similarly in verse 3, where we read : ' Thou Lord, Almighty, didst create all things for Thy Name's sake ; and didst give food and drink to men for their enjoyment, that they might give thanks to Thee '; the Christian note comes in in what almost reads like an addition : ' but us hast Thou blest with spiritual food and drink and eternal light through Thy Servant '.

In reading these passages from the *Didaché*, then, which echo those of the early Christian Liturgy, one cannot fail to be impressed by the Jewish tone and atmosphere of them. They witness, therefore, to Jewish liturgical influence upon early Christian forms of worship.

We may note, lastly, as far as the *Didaché* is concerned, the words at the end of chap. x : ' But suffer the prophets to give thanks as much as they will.' One may gather from this that, while the subject-matter of prayer and thanksgiving was more or less

---

[1] See further below, pp. 198 f.

stereotyped, the actual wording and the length were
left to the leader or 'prophet'. That this usage was
taken over from the Jewish Church can scarcely be
doubted in view of what we have seen to have been
the custom of the Synagogue in early days. This, of
course, does not mean that there were no fixed forms of
prayer in the early Jewish Liturgy, for we have just seen
that one, at least, of such existed in pre-Christian times;
that there were both fixed and *extempore* prayers on
different occasions is very natural. But whatever the
form of prayer in the Jewish Church, the times of
offering them, which in the Synagogue followed the
times of the sacrificial offerings of the Temple Service,
were fixed; and this usage seems to be reflected when,
in chap. viii. 2, 3 of the *Didaché*, the direction is given
that the Lord's Prayer is to be said three times a day.

We must refer next to *Justin Martyr*. In his
First Apology and in the *Dialogue with Trypho* there
are some passages in which liturgical details are dealt
with; in these some marks of Jewish influence are to
be discerned with regard to the subject of Prayer and
Thanksgiving.

In his account of the introductory portion of the
weekly Sunday Eucharist he makes mention of the
prayers in which all present took part, standing:
ἔπειτα ἀνιστάμεθα κοινῇ πάντες καὶ εὐχὰς πέμπομεν (*Apol.*
i. 67); this immediately precedes the Eucharist proper.
When it is realized that this introductory part of the
Service contains precisely the elements which formed
the synagogal liturgy, we may justifiably believe that
the prayers to which Justin here refers were based on
those of the *Shemôneh 'Esreh* among others. This
belief is strengthened by the fact that when in another
passage, Justin not only refers to prayer (this time in

the Eucharist proper), but indicates its content, we are able to discern distinct marks of Jewish influence. This passage is in the *Dialogue* xli, where, in reference to the eucharistic prayer, Justin says that it was Christ's desire that we should also thank God for having created the world, with all that is in it, for man's benefit, as well as for having freed him from the bondage of sin in which men were living. We shall point out later (pp. 184 ff., below) that this conjunction of the two thoughts of Creation and Redemption are just those which figure prominently in *Kiddûsh*. And if, as we shall endeavour to show in Chap. VI, *Kiddûsh* formed the background, as far as the form was concerned, of the words of consecration, it would explain where Justin got the idea that it was Christ's desire that thanksgiving for the Creation should be uttered during the eucharistic prayer. Thanksgiving for redemption from sin would naturally enough correspond to that for deliverance from the Egyptian bondage which occurs in *Kiddûsh*.

We may point, in passing, to the mark of Jewish influence to be discerned again in the *extempore* form of prayer mentioned by Justin ; for it is in reference to the eucharistic prayer that he says : . . . εὐχὰς ὁμοίως καὶ εὐχαριστίας, ὅση δύναμις αὐτῷ ἀναπέμπει (*Apol.* i. 67).

But to return to the *Shemôneh 'Esreh* ; another illustration of the way in which this prayer set the pattern for the liturgical prayers of the Church may be seen on comparing the thirteenth Benediction, which contains intercessory petitions for the members and officials of the congregation, with a passage from *Sarapion's Liturgy*. The Benediction runs as follows : [1]

---

[1] For the distinction between the earlier and later portions of this Benediction, see above, pp. 59 ff.

Upon the righteous and upon the pious, upon the elders of Thy people the house of Israel, upon the remnant of their scribes, and upon the proselytes of righteousness, let Thy mercies be stirred, O Lord our God ; and grant a good reward unto all that trust in Thy Name in truth ; and set out our portion with them for ever ; let us not be ashamed, for in Thy Name have we trusted, and we have relied upon Thy salvation. Blessed art Thou, O Lord, the Stay and the Trust of the righteous.

Compare with this the following passage from *Sarapion's Liturgy* :

'On Thee do we call, Saviour and Lord, the God of all flesh and Lord of all spirits, the Blessed One, the Giver of every blessing. Sanctify this bishop, keep him from every temptation, and grant him wisdom and understanding, yea, grant that he may make good progress in Thy knowledge. We pray to Thee also for his fellow-elders ("presbyters") ; sanctify them, give them wisdom, understanding, and the true doctrine ; grant that they may teach Thy holy truths rightly and blamelessly. Sanctify also the deacons, that they may be pure in heart and body, and serve Thee with a pure conscience that they may stand in the presence of Thy Body and Thy holy Blood. We pray to Thee also for the sub-deacons, the readers, and the interpreters.' [1]

Intercession is made, further, for all who serve the Church ; for hermits, for all who are married, and for children.

Although there are no verbal correspondences here, yet the essence of each is the same, intercession for the religious leaders and the faithful members of the Church. Prayers for them occur in all the eastern liturgies.

[1] Wobbermin, *Altchristliche liturgische Stücke*, pp. 17 ff.

We have seen that intercessions for rulers were offered in the Jewish Church; this is enjoined in 1 Tim. ii. 1 f   In the liturgical prayer in 1 *Clement*, already quoted, there is a passage in which prayer is offered for rulers : 'Thou, Master, gavest the authority of the Kingdom to them ... to them, Lord, grant health, peace, concord, firmness, that they may administer the government which Thou hast given them without offence . . . do Thou, O Lord, direct their counsels according to that which is good and pleasing in Thy sight, that they may administer in peace and meekness, with piety, the authority which hath been given them by Thee, and find mercy in Thine eyes.' See also Justin Martyr, *Apol.* i. 17, and Tertullian, *Apol.* xxx.

A characteristic of synagogal prayer was confession of sin and prayer for forgiveness. For example, the sixth Benediction of the *Shemôneh 'Esreh* runs :

Forgive us, our Father, for we have sinned ;
Pardon us, our King, for we have transgressed.
For Thou art the God of goodness, Thou dost forgive.
Blessed art Thou, O Lord, who art gracious, and dost abundantly forgive.

In the liturgical prayer in 1 *Clement* this characteristic also occurs :

'. . . O merciful and compassionate, forgive us our iniquities and unrighteous acts and transgressions and shortcomings. Reckon not every sin of Thy servants and handmaidens, but cleanse us with the cleansing of Thy truth, and guide our steps to walk in holiness of heart, to do the things that are beautiful and well-pleasing in Thy sight (lx. 1)'.

Of many other examples we may take the following extract from the *Liturgy of Sarapion* :

'Prostrate before Thee, O loving God, we confess

our weaknesses, and pray for Thy strength to help us. Forgive us our past sins, and pass over former errors, and make us a new people ; yea, make us holy and pure servants. Unto Thee do we commend ourselves ; receive us, O God of truth ; accept Thy people and sanctify them wholly ; grant that they may walk blamelessly and in purity. . . .'

Finally, we give one or two illustrations of the doxology which usually concludes a prayer, for this, too, was adopted by the Church from the synagogal pattern. In the prayers cited above (p. 54) from the Jewish Liturgy various forms of doxology occur ; particularly noticeable is the way in which each section of the *Shemôneh 'Esreh* concludes with a doxology. In the Christian prayers the doxology is generally, as is natural, connected with the name of Jesus Christ ; thus, the liturgical prayer in 1 *Clement* concludes with the words : ' O Thou who art alone able to do these things, and more abundantly excellent things, for us, unto Thee do we give praise through the High-priest and Guardian of our souls, Jesus Christ, through whom be glory and majesty to Thee, both now, and unto all generations, and unto all eternity (lxi. 3)'. Again, in the *Didaché* (x. 4), the abbreviated eucharistic prayer ends with the words : 'Above all, we give thanks to Thee for that Thou art mighty. To Thee be glory for ever.'

Examples of this kind will be found in all the early liturgical prayers of the Church ; it is unnecessary to give further extracts. The main point to emphasize is that the prayers of the Synagogue furnished the pattern which was adopted by the Church.

(*b*) It is more than probable that other prayers of the pre-Christian synagogal Liturgy were, in essence, taken over by the Church; but to offer details of this by giving the relevant passages from the early Christian liturgies in full (which would be necessary in order to realize the extent of Jewish influence), and comparing them with the prayers cited in Chap. II, would take up a great deal of space. We must content ourselves with suggesting to those whom it may interest that they should compare the following synagogal prayers with the passages indicated from the Liturgy of the eighth book of the *Apostolic Constitutions* (the 'Clementine' Liturgy), published by Brightman, *Op. cit.*, pp. 3 ff.; we believe that they will not fail to see how both the Jewish and Christian material belong fundamentally to the same mould :

With *Yôtzer* (see p. 48, above) compare the passage beginning, Σὺ γάρ, Θεὲ αἰώνιε . . . (Brightman, p. 15, line 7). With *'Ahabah* (see pp. 48, 49, above) compare the passage beginning, ἀρωγὲ δυνατὲ . . . (Brightman, p. 12, line 22). With *Geullah* (see p. 50, above) compare the passage beginning, σὺ Κύριε Ἑβραίους . . . (Brightman, p. 18, line 5). These are not the only passages, by any means, in which the influence of synagogal prayers is to be discerned; but they offer good instances. With regard to *Geullah*, however, one other illustration may be given. We pointed out (see p. 50) that one part of this prayer formed the basis of an early liturgical Christian prayer. In several of the synagogal prayers mention is made of the deliverance from the Egyptian bondage; this has always been regarded in the Jewish Church as the outstanding mark of God's mercy to His people, and is frequently spoken of as the great act of Divine redemption. In the early Christian Church that which corresponded to this was the redemption from darkness and sin wrought by

Jesus Christ. Bearing this in mind, a comparison between the two following passages will show, we maintain, how this element, which is so pronounced in *Geullah*, was borrowed and adapted by the Christian Church.

The passage from *Geullah* ('Redemption') runs thus :

> From Egypt didst Thou redeem us, O Lord our God, and from the house of bondage didst Thou deliver us. All their firstborn didst Thou slay; but Thy firstborn didst Thou redeem. Thou didst divide the Red Sea, and the arrogant didst Thou drown. But Thy beloved ones didst Thou cause to pass through; and the waters covered their adversaries; not one of them was left. Wherefore the beloved praised and extolled God, and the chosen ones offered hymns, songs, praises, blessings, and thanksgivings to the King—God who liveth and endureth, who is high and exalted, great and awe-inspiring (נורא); who bringeth low the haughty, and setteth on high the meek; who leadeth forth the bound, and redeemeth the lowly; who helpeth the poor, and answereth His people when they cry unto him. Praises to God Most High ; blessed be He, yea blessed.

With this we compare 1 *Clem.* lix :

> '. . . but we shall be innocent of this sin, and will pray with eager entreaty and supplication that the Creator of all things may guard unhurt the number of His chosen numbered in all the world through His beloved Servant Jesus Christ, through whom He called us from darkness to light, from ignorance to the knowledge of His glorious Name. [Grant us, Lord,] to hope on Thy Name, supreme source of all creation ; open the eyes of our hearts to know Thee the only Highest in the highest, who remainest holy among the holy ; who humblest the pride of the haughty, who destroyest the imaginings of the nations, who dost set up the meek on high, who dost humble the

lofty, who makest rich and makest poor, who killest and makest alive, who alone art the Finder[1] of spirits, and God of all flesh; who dost look into the abysses, and beholdest the works of man, who art the Helper of those in danger, the Saviour of those without hope, the Creator and Overseer of every spirit; who multipliest the nations on earth, and hast chosen out from them all those that love Thee through Jesus Christ Thy beloved Servant; through Him hast Thou taught us, and sanctified us, and brought us to honour. We beseech Thee, Master, to be our help and succour. Save those of us who are in affliction, have mercy on the humble, raise the fallen, manifest Thyself to the needy, heal the sick, turn back them that err of Thy people, feed the hungry, ransom our prisoners, raise up the weak, comfort the faint-hearted; let all nations know Thee, that Thou alone art God, and that Jesus Christ is Thy Servant, and that we are Thy people and the sheep of Thy pasture. . . .'

Even a cursory comparison of these two passages shows their close relationship, while a closer examination reveals so many points of contact and identity of thought that it is impossible not to see that the latter is an adaptation of the former. In this case it is something more than a question of one influencing the other; and when it is realized how the echoes of this christianized Jewish prayer resound in all the ancient Liturgies, the indebtedness of the Church for many of her forms of prayer to the Synagogue will be readily granted.

(*c*) Another synagogal prayer concerning which a word must be said here is '*Alenu* (' It is meet for us', see p. 68, above). It is an open question as to whether that portion of '*Alenu* to be quoted was in part adopted by the Church; but the possibility is

---

[1] Or, ' Benefactor ', according to another reading.

certainly there, for which reason it is worth while drawing attention to it. This prayer was said at the conclusion of the daily Synagogue services; a considerable part of it has already been given, but not that part of it which contains a prayer for the heathen nations, that they may be converted and turn from their wickedness and acknowledge the One God, viz.:

Therefore we hope in Thee, O Lord our God, that we may speedily see the glory of Thy might,

When Thou removest the abominations from the earth, and the idols shall be utterly cut off;

When the world shall be set right in the Kingdom of the Almighty; and all the children of flesh shall call upon Thy Name.

When Thou wilt turn unto Thyself all the wicked of the earth, that all the inhabitants of the world may perceive and know

That to Thee every knee must bow, every tongue swear.

Before Thee, O Lord our God, let them bow and fall down; and to the glory of Thy Great Name, let them give honour.

And let them take upon themselves the yoke of Thy Kingdom, and do Thou reign over them for ever and ever.

For the Kingdom is Thine, and for ever and ever shalt Thou reign in glory.

In reference to this Kohler says:

'Singularly enough, in the early Christian Church, converts, before being baptized, had to step forward at the end of divine service, and make public confession by first turning backward, renouncing the kingdom of Satan, and spitting out as a sign of contempt; then turning forward in the name of the Creator of the world and of man, they took the oath of allegiance to Jesus as the Son of God (see Höfling, *Taufe*,[1] i. 381; Cyril, *De Mysteriis*, i. 2). Possibly the prayer for the

---

[1] *Das Sacrament der Taufe*, 2 vols. (1846–8).

conversion of all heathen nations, contained in the latter portion of the *'Alenu,* has some connexion with the practice adopted by the Church of admitting proselytes at the end of the service.'[1]

Kohler's suggestion is much to the point, especially when it is remembered that the rite of Baptism (*Tebilah*) was necessary for proselytes to Judaism in pre-Christian times,[2] and that the renunciation of Satan at Christian Baptism coincided precisely with the insistence on leading a moral life henceforth, which was a condition for Gentile proselytes to Judaism. 'The Jewish synagogue', says Harnack, 'had already drawn up a catechism for proselytes and made morality the condition of religion; it had already *instituted a training* for religion. Christianity took this up and deepened it. In so doing it was actuated by the very strongest motives, for otherwise it could not protect itself against the varied forms of "idolatry" or realize its cherished ideal of being the *holy* church of God.'[3]

(*d*) We have seen that the *Kedûshah* ('Sanctification,' i. e. of the Name), which was in very early days attached to the third Benediction of the *Shemôneh 'Esreh,* occurs in three parts of the Jewish Liturgy, thus showing the importance attached to it. In its original form it was shorter than the form now used in the Synagogue; but that it was said antiphonally long before the beginning of the Christian era does not admit of doubt.

The appropriateness of the *Kedûshah* after the third *Shemôneh 'Esreh* Benediction will be seen from the following; the Benediction runs:

---

[1] *JE* i. 338 *a*.   [2] See further on this, *RWS*[2], pp. 281 ff.
[3] *The Mission and Expansion of Christianity,* i. 391 f. (1908).

Thou art holy, and holy is Thy Name
And holy ones praise Thee every day, (Selah).[1]
Blessed art Thou, O Lord, the Holy God.

Then follows the *Kedûshah*, which we give in its present form, for although there is no doubt that it was originally shorter, it cannot have been very much shorter because its present length is not great ; it is said antiphonally, thus :

Reader : We will sanctify Thy Name in the world even as they sanctify it in the highest heavens, as it is written by the hand of Thy prophet :
  And they cried one to the other and said,
Congregation : Holy, holy, holy, is the Lord of hosts ; the whole earth is full of His glory (Isa. vi. 3).
Reader : To those over against them they say, Blessed—
Congregation : Blessed be the glory of the Lord from His place (Ezek. iii. 12).
Reader : And in Thy holy words it is written, saying,
Congregation : The Lord shall reign for ever, thy God, O Zion, unto all generations. Praise ye the Lord (Ps. cxlvi. 10).
Reader : Unto all generations we will declare Thy greatness, and to eternity we will hallow Thy holiness ; and Thy praise, O our God, shall never depart from our mouth, for a great and holy God and King art Thou. Blessed art Thou, O Lord, the holy God.

In the developed angelology of Judaism, which arose through Persian influence, it was taught that innumerable hosts of angels were ever worshipping God in Heaven. This is reflected, e. g. in Dan. vii. 10 : 'thousand thousands ministered unto him, and ten thousand times ten thousand stood before him.' From this to the thought that when men worshipped God on

---

[1] This, now meaningless, word is still said ; its presence is an infallible sign of antiquity.

earth they were joined by the angels in heaven, was a very natural one ; and the *Kedûshah* gives expression to this.

The recitation in the Synagogue by the first Jewish Christians of the *Kedûshah* ensured its continuance in Christian worship after their final withdrawal from the Jewish Church ; hence we find in the earliest records of specifically Christian worship the mention of the *Trisagion* as it came to be called. Thus in 1 *Clem.* xxxiv. 5 ff. it says :

'Let our glorifying and confidence be in Him ; let us be subject to His will ; let us consider the whole multitude of His angels, how they stand ready and minister to His will. For the Scripture saith, "Ten thousand times ten thousand stood by Him, and thousand thousands ministered unto Him", and they cried, "Holy, Holy, Holy is the Lord Sabaoth, the whole creation is full of His glory". Therefore, we too must be gathered together with one accord in our conscience, and cry earnestly unto Him, as it were, with one mouth, that we may be partakers of His great and glorious promises. . . .'

Public worship is clearly referred to here as the words 'we too must be gathered together' show ; so that it is evident from this passage that the *Trisagion* was used in the worship of the Church in these early days ; and the phrase 'as it were with one mouth' implies that the congregation took part in saying, or more probably singing, it.

The reference in Pliny's *Letter to Trajan* to the antiphonal (*secum invicem*) singing of a hymn (*carmen*) when the Christians gathered together before dawn on a fixed day (*stato die*, presumably the first day of the week), may conceivably refer to the *Trisagion*. Opinions differ, it is true, on the question as to whether the gathering together of which Pliny writes refers to the Eucharist or not. He mentions in the same letter the 'common and harmless meal' (. . . *cibum, promiscuum tamen et innoxium*) which takes place later in the day. Some maintain that this latter was the Eucharist;[1] others understand it to refer to the *Agapé*. Lightfoot gives reasons for holding the view that it was the *Agapé*; he believes that this was separated from the Eucharist, which was celebrated at the early service, before the time of Trajan's edict, and refers to the evidence of Tertullian, *De Cor.* 3: *Eucharistiae sacramentum . . . antelucanis coetibus . . . sumimus.*[2] If Lightfoot and others are right in their belief that the gathering together before dawn refers to the Eucharist, then the hymn or song spoken of by Pliny may well have been the *Trisagion*; as *the* hymn of glory to God, and as the earliest hymn of the Church, it was certainly the most important; this, added to the fact that Pliny speaks of it as having been sung antiphonally, makes it reasonable to think that it may have been the *Trisagion*[3] with which we have here to do.

It is fortunate that in 1 *Clement* we have a distinct reference to the *Trisagion* as an element in public worship, for, apart from what is said in Pliny's letter, the evidence of which is uncertain so far as the *Trisagion* is concerned, we have no further mention of it until we come to the time of Clement of Alex-

[1] E. g. Srawley, *The Early History of the Liturgy*, p. 33 (1913).

[2] *Op. cit.*, Part ii, vol. i, p. 52 ; he refers to Harnack who 'advocates the view that the separation was due to the edict of Trajan'.

[3] Psalms, it is true, were also sung antiphonally in the Jewish Church and, presumably therefore, by the early Christians; but these were not used at the Eucharist proper, but only at the preparatory service; we assume that the Eucharist proper is spoken of here.

andria, who, though he does not quote it, makes a quite obvious reference to it when, in speaking of the Eucharist, he says: 'giving thanks to God always, as the creatures which gave glory to God in Isaiah's allegory.'[1] Tertullian also refers to it, speaking of it as the *Sanctus*,[2] the first to apply this name to it; he also speaks of the angels singing it in another passage.[3]

There seems to be a reference to the *Trisagion* in Origen's *Contra Cels.* viii. 34:[4] 'And if we wish to have also a multitude of those we desire to find loving, we learn that thousand thousands stood before Him, and ten thousand times ten thousand ministered unto Him, and these, regarding as their kinsmen and friends those who imitate their piety towards God . . .' It is also mentioned by Cyril of Jerusalem, *Cat. Myst.* v. 3, where it is quoted in full. But though the evidence of the use of this synagogal hymn of praise in the worship of the Christian Church is less than one might expect, it is sufficient to show that it *was* used; and when we come to the earliest Liturgies we find in them ample proof of this. One or two examples will fully suffice because it is well known that all the great Liturgies from the fifth century onwards contain it. In the *Apostolic Constitutions* (the Clementine), towards the end of the long thanksgiving come the words: 'Innumerable hosts of angels and archangels . . . praise Thee . . .'; then follows the direction: 'And let all the people say together', and it continues:

'Holy, Holy, Holy, Lord Sabaôth,
Heaven and earth are full of His glory;
Blessed be He for ever. Amen.'[5]

---

[1] *Strom.* vii. 12, Migne, *PG* ix, col. 511.   [2] *De Spectac.* xxv.
[3] *De Orat.* iii.   [4] Quoted by Brightman, *Op. cit.*, p. 508.
[5] This peculiarly characteristic Jewish Benediction is worth noting.

Similarly, in the corresponding prayer in *Sarapion's Liturgy*, reference is made to the myriads of angels and archangels ministering in heaven, with whom the worshippers on earth join in saying : ' Holy, Holy, Holy, Lord Sabaôth ; heaven and earth are full of Thy glory.' There is not so much detail as in the *Apostolic Constitutions*, but Sarapion is clearly only giving a general summary, not a detailed account of the service.

Further illustrations are unnecessary. It may be claimed from what has been said that the *Kedûshah* of the Synagogue Liturgy is the source to which we must look for the origin of the *Trisagion* in the Christian Liturgy.

IV. THE AMEN.

The congregational response of *Amen* at the conclusion of a prayer to denote participation and emphasis is such an obvious matter that it may seem unnecessary to dilate further upon it. Nevertheless, the great insistence upon it in the Synagogue worship, which shows the importance attached to it, and its consequent adoption by the Christian Church, makes it worth while to offer a few illustrations of its use in early Christian worship.

St. Paul takes for granted that it is said, but he insists on its *intelligent* utterance (1 Cor. xiv. 16 ; cp. 2 Cor. i. 20) ; he who said *Amen* meant thereby that he associated himself with what had been said by another.[1] The earliest known liturgical prayer of the

[1] Different, of course, is the use of ἀμήν ἀμήν in the Gospels ; this is peculiar to Christ, and is not in accordance with Hebrew or Aramaic usage, see Dalman, *Die Worte Jesu*, pp. 186 ff. (1898); it is used in a special way in the Apocalypse, e. g. i. 7, xxii. 21.

Church concludes with it (1 *Clem.* lxi. 3), so, too, in the *Didaché* x. 6 ; Justin Martyr makes special mention of the congregational *Amen* at the end of the Eucharistic prayer (*Apol.* i. 67), and in the same way Clement of Alexandria (*Stromateis* vi. 14); many other references to it occur, but it is unnecessary to multiply examples.

Just as in the Synagogue usage the *Amen* concluded the doxology with which the prayer ended, so in the Christian Church it came after the name of Christ uttered at the end of the prayer which was offered through Him. A special significance attached to the congregational *Amen* after the Consecration prayer, as well as its utterance after receiving the sacred elements; we do not read of the latter in the earliest periods. Our particular concern here, however, is to point to the use of the *Amen* as a further instance of the influence of the Synagogue worship on that of the early Church.

V. PSALMS.

The words in 1 Cor. xiv. 26 (cp. also Eph. v. 19 ; Col. iii. 16): 'When ye come together, each hath a psalm . . .', are sufficient to show that in the Gentile churches the liturgical use of psalms was customary from the beginning ; and this can only have been adopted from the Jewish Church. Apart from the New Testament, however, but little light is thrown on the liturgical use of psalms in our earliest sources. At the same time, the frequent quotations from them in the writings of the Apostolic Fathers shows great familiarity with them, and this would doubtless, in part, be due to the recitation and singing of them in public worship. At any rate, from what is said on the subject in slightly later sources it is evident that psalms had always been used in Christian worship, and that, therefore, the

Jewish liturgical use of them had been continued uninterruptedly by the Christian Church.

Thus, Tertullian, who is the first post-biblical Christian writer to mention the liturgical use of psalms, in describing the service on the first day of the week, says, among other things, that 'psalms are sung' (*De Anima* ix). Again, in the *Apostolic Constitutions* ii. 59, in the pro-anaphoral part of the Liturgy, after the reading of ·the Old Testament lessons 'the hymns of David' are sung, and the people sing the antiphons.

VI. CONFESSION.

As has already been pointed out, confession was a characteristic element in many of the prayers of the Jewish Liturgy and of early Christian forms of prayer. But in addition to this, as we saw in Chap. II, § viii, there were special ancient forms of confession in the Temple and, later, in the Synagogue Liturgy. When we turn to the earliest forms of Christian worship we find a similar usage.

In 1 *Clem.* lii. 1 it is said : 'The Master, brethren, is in need of nothing ; He asks nothing of anyone, save that confession be made to Him'; this is followed by a quotation of Ps. lxix. 30 ff. ; l. 14, 15 ; li. 17.

Congregational confession is definitely enjoined in *Did.* xiv. 1 : 'On the Lord's Day of the Lord, being assembled, break bread and offer the Eucharist, after confessing your transgressions that your offering may be pure.'[1] In iv. 14 it is said : 'In the congregation thou shalt confess thy transgressions, and thou shalt not give thyself to this prayer with an evil conscience.'

[1] Mal. i. 11, which together with verse 14, quoted in the context, is frequently interpreted in reference to the Eucharist, e. g. Justin Mart., *Dial. with Tryp.* xxviii, &c.

It was pointed out above (p. 78) that the form of confession called *Ashamnu*, of the Synagogue Liturgy, was alphabetic ; there is reason to believe that in the early Church a confession in similar form was used.[1]

The subject of confession is so often referred to by early Church writers,[2] and is so well known as an element in the fully developed liturgies of the Church, that it is not necessary to give further details here ; our object being to point to the extreme probability of the Christian Church having adopted it from the Synagogue Liturgy.

VII. The Decalogue.

It has been shown above that the recitation of the Decalogue, following that of the *Shema'*, was customary in the Synagogue service—it followed here, doubtless, the Temple Liturgy—and that therefore the assumption is justified that the first Jewish Christians did the same ; indeed, this is practically proved by the fact that the Synagogue abrogated the liturgical use of the Decalogue ' on account of the cavilling of the heretics ', i.e. Christians.   If this was so, however, the custom must have ceased at an early period ; for it does not appear, as far as can be ascertained, that any trace of the liturgical use of the Decalogue is to be discovered in any early Christian Liturgy.[3]   Blunt[4] says : ' The use of the Ten Commandments in the Communion Service is quite peculiar to the English Church.   It

[1] See Rendel Harris, *The Teaching of the Apostles*, pp. 82 ff. (1887).

[2] E. g. Origen, *Hom. in Lev.* ii. 4 (Migne, *PG* xii. 418) ; Tertullian, *De Pœnit.* ix ; see also Introd. to Hermas's *Mandata* ; *Apos. Const.* ii. 22.

[3] The references to the Decalogue in *Did.* ii and *Barn.* xix do not offer any evidence for its liturgical use.

[4] *The Annotated Book of Common Prayer*, p. 166 (1872).

is probably derived from the custom of reciting and expounding them at certain intervals, which is so frequently enjoined by the ancient Synods and the Bishops of the Church of England.' In view of what has been said it is just possible that there is a primitive Church precedent for the use of the Anglican Church here.

VIII. The Lord's Prayer.

The doxology added to the Lord's Prayer[1] would of itself be sufficient evidence to show that it was incorporated in the Liturgy from the earliest times. It is not, however, within our province to follow out here the history of the liturgical use of the Lord's Prayer. The reason for devoting a brief space to its consideration is to show in how far it may be regarded as being based on elements in the synagogal liturgy familiar to the disciples of our Lord. Parallels in early Rabbinical literature are abundant;[2] but as the source of these is, in all probability, the Jewish Liturgy we are not concerned with them here.[3]

The address 'Our Father' (*'Abinu*) occurs, e.g. in the fifth and sixth Benedictions of the *Shemôneh 'Esreh* and in the *'Ahabah* prayer.[4]

---

[1] 'That the true text of St. Matthew's Gospel had no doxology at the close of the Lord's Prayer cannot be considered doubtful' (Chase, *The Lord's Prayer in the Early Church*, in 'Texts and Studies' i. 3 [1891]). See further, Westcott and Hort, *The New Testament in the Original Greek*, ii, Notes on Select Readings, pp. 8 ff. (1882).

[2] See, for example, Taylor, *Op. cit.*, pp. 124 ff.; Klein, *Der aelteste christliche Katechismus*, pp. 256 ff. (1909).

[3] In *Tos. Ber.* iii. 7 there are several instances of prayers composed by Rabbis, but they are all based on familiar liturgical prayers.

[4] For the full phrase, 'Our Father which art in Heaven,' see, for example, Mishnah, *Aboth* v. 23, *Ber.* v. 1, *Yoma* iii. 9.

The next three phrases are all contained, if not verbally certainly in essence, in the opening sentences of *Kaddish*:

'. . . Hallowed be His great *Name* in the world which He created according to His *will*. May He establish His *Kingdom* . . .'; the thoughts of the hallowing of the Name and the coming of the Kingdom occur also in *Kedushah* : 'We will sanctify Thy Name in the world even as they sanctify it in the highest heavens. . . . The Lord shall reign for ever.' We may compare also two other Benedictions, but one cannot attach the same importance to these because there is not sufficient evidence to prove them to be pre-Christian, though one must recognize the probability of their being so. Among the morning Benedictions belonging to the introductory portion of the daily service occurs one which runs thus :

'Our Father which art in Heaven, show mercy towards us for Thy great Name's sake whereby we are called ;[1] and fulfil unto us, O Lord our God, that which hath been written, At that time will I bring you in, and at that time will I gather you . . .'

This last sentence refers to the coming of the Kingdom. In the preceding supplication occur the words : 'Sanctify Thy Name upon them that sanctify it, yea, sanctify Thy Name throughout Thy world.'

The other is one of the Benedictions in the evening service :

'Our God, which art in Heaven, assert the unity of Thy Name, and establish Thy Kingdom continually, and reign over us for ever and ever.'

For the petition, 'Give us this day our daily bread',

[1] *Lit.* 'Thy great Name which is called over us'; the phrase comes from Deut. xxviii. 10.

there is no real parallel in the Jewish Liturgy ; the only passage which is in some sense reminiscent of it is in the ninth Benediction of the *Shemôneh 'Esreh* :

'. . . Satisfy the world and its fulness with Thy goodness. And give plenty upon the face of the earth through the richness of the gifts of Thy hands . . .'

On the other hand, the sixth Benediction of the *Shemôneh 'Esreh* may, in part, well lie behind the petition, ' Forgive us . . .' ; it runs :

' Forgive us, our Father, for we have sinned ;
Pardon us, our King, for we have transgressed ;
For Thou art the God of goodness, Thou dost forgive . . .'

But the one very striking difference will at once be noticed, viz. there is no *condition* of forgiveness such as seems to be implied in the petition of the Lord's Prayer. Abrahams says that if, as he believes, there is some sort of conditional connexion established between man's forgiveness and God's in this petition, then we have in it one ' which is altogether without Jewish parallel '. A little further on he says :

' Jesus could be very exacting in the light of his teaching on forgiveness of man by man. Moreover, if the Son of Man has power to forgive (Matt. ix. 6 ; Mk. ii. 10 ; Lk. v. 4), then in a sense God Himself forgives through man (cp. Eph. iv. 32), not through man's intermediation, but through man's exemplification of the divine mercy. This would involve a *nuance* unfamiliar if not unknown to Jewish theology. All these considerations suggest the conclusion that this particular petition in the Lord's Prayer emanates, not from Jewish models, but from the peculiar thought from Jesus himself.' [1]

[1] *Studies in Pharisaism and the Gospels* (Second Series), pp. 96 ff. (1924) ; the whole essay from which the words are quoted is admirable.

Finally, we have the last two petitions. For these there is a distinct parallelism in one of the Benedictions for the daily Morning Service; but, as already pointed out, there is insufficient evidence for proving its pre-Christian origin, while granting the probability that this may be so. They are as follows:

'O lead us not into the power of sin, or of transgression or iniquity, or of temptation, or of scorn.'

'May it be Thy will, O Lord my God, and God of my fathers, to deliver me this day, and every day, from arrogant men and from arrogance . . . and from any mishap, and from the adversary that destroyeth.'

.   .   .   .

The illustrations of the marks of Jewish liturgical influence on early forms of Christian worship given in this somewhat lengthy chapter may not be exhaustive; but at least it is hoped that they are sufficient to prove the reality of that influence.

PART III
SPECIAL STUDIES

VI

THE ANTECEDENTS OF THE EUCHARIST

I

For reasons which will appear later it is necessary to insist upon the fact that the institution of the Eucharist took place during, probably more precisely at the end of, a meal. In regard to this all the four Gospel narratives are in agreement. The importance of this for our subsequent discussion is such that it will be well to cite the relevant passages:

Matt. xxvi. 20: . . . *Now when even was come, he was sitting at meat with the twelve disciples ; and as they were eating, he said, Verily I say unto you, that one of you shall betray me.* Then follows the question, *Is it I ?* the dipping of the sop, and the reply of Christ to Judas, *Thou hast said.* Not until verse 26 come the words : *And as they were eating Jesus took bread . . .* So that the meal must have been proceeding for some time before the institution took place. Immediately after it they sang a hymn and went out unto the Mount of Olives ; it looks, therefore, as though the institution did not take place until the *conclusion* of the meal.

Mk. xiv. 18: . . . *And as they sat and were eating, Jesus said, Verily I say unto you, One of you shall betray me . . .* Then in verse 22 it continues : *And as they were eating he took bread . . .* As in the Matthaean account, they go out immediately after a hymn had been sung.

Luke xxii. 14 . . . : Here it is a little different, but
the main point is the same : *And when the hour was
come, he sat down, and the apostles with him.   And he
said unto them, With desire I have desired to eat this
passover with you before I suffer . . .   And he received
a cup, and, when he had given thanks, he said . . .   And
he took bread, and when he had given thanks . . .*

The account makes it clear that the institution did
not take place until some time after the meal had
begun.   It is of importance to note the mention of the
cup before that of the bread.   This will be referred to
again later.

The fourth Gospel (xiii. 1 ff. to be quoted presently)
is in accordance with the Synoptists on this point.

It is quite clear, therefore, that according to the
accounts in all the four Gospels the institution of the
Lord's Supper took place either during or, more probably, after a meal ; so that, apart from the significance
of this fact in view of what will be said later, it will be
realized that, so far as the words of consecration are
concerned, there can be no question of a grace before
meals.

II

If, then, a meal was being partaken of before the
institution took place, or if the meal was completed
before it took place, the question suggests itself as to
what this meal was ; and the answer which, of course,
immediately rises to our lips is : the Passover meal.
But there are some weighty considerations which go to
show that it was *not* a Passover meal.   This demands
some attention, for the contention that it was not a
Passover meal runs counter to a good deal that we
read in the Gospels ; and it has always been taken for

granted that the Last Supper took place during such a meal.

(*a*) It is well known that there is a serious discrepancy between the Synoptic accounts of the Last Supper and that of the fourth Gospel. Let us make this clear.

According to the fourth Gospel the Last Supper took place *before* the Passover feast, on the Day of Preparation. That was Nisan 14, the day on which the paschal lambs were sacrificed in the Temple. The following passages will show this :

John xiii. 1 ff. *Now before the feast of the Passover, Jesus knowing that his hour was come that he should depart out of this world unto the Father . . . and during supper . . .* Then comes the washing of the disciples' feet, the discourse on this example of humility, and the continuation of the meal and the dipping of the sop ; after that the departure of Judas. The Last Supper is thus clearly stated to have taken place *before* the Passover, and therefore the meal could not have been the Passover feast. But in this chapter there is one passage in which it says almost in so many words that this was not a Passover feast. This is in verses 27 ff. :
. . . Jesus therefore saith unto him, that thou doest, do quickly. Now no man at the table knew for what intent he spake this unto him. For some thought, because Judas had the bag, that Jesus said unto him, Buy what things we have need of for the feast . . . Those words are quite decisive ; for if the disciples thought that Judas had gone out to buy things for the feast, it is obvious that they could not have been partaking of the feast at the time ! The festival could not even have begun ; for it was impossible to buy anything during the feast ;

for during it buying and selling were forbidden by the Law. Again:

John xviii. 28: *They lead Jesus therefore from Caiaphas into the palace: and it was early; and they themselves entered not into the palace, that they might not be defiled, but might eat the Passover.* On the face of it this took place after the Last Supper, and yet the eating of the Passover is still to come.

John xix. 14: *Now it was the Preparation of the Passover; it was about the sixth hour; and he* [Pilate] *saith unto the Jews, Behold your King!* The Day of Preparation was Nisan 14, which began at 6 p.m. on the Thursday, and lasted till 6 p.m. on the Friday; this was therefore about midday on the Friday; the first day of the Passover festival would begin at 6 p.m. on that day. Further,

John xix. 31: *The Jews, therefore, because it was the Preparation, that the bodies should not remain upon the Cross upon the sabbath (for the day of that sabbath was a high day) asked of Pilate that their legs might be broken, and that they might be taken away.* The sabbath was a high day because this year it fell on the first day of the feast of the Passover; both would begin at 6 p.m. that evening; so that here again we see that the feast proper had not yet begun, it was only the Preparation; the great mass of the people were in the Temple where the paschal lambs were being sacrificed in preparation for the feast; it was still Nisan 14. And lastly,

John xix. 42: *There then, because of the Jews' Preparation (for the tomb was nigh at hand) they laid Jesus.* Our Lord is, therefore, laid in the tomb before the Passover feast begins.

From these five passages then in the fourth Gospel it is quite clear that (1) the Last Supper took place on the day *before* the feast of the Passover ; therefore it could not have been the Passover meal during which, or after which, the institution of the Eucharist took place ; and (2) the Crucifixion was on the day of the Preparation of the Passover, Nisan 14, the day on which the Passover lambs were sacrificed.

The following table of dates will help to make this quite clear :

Nisan 14, i.e. 6 p.m. on Thursday to 6 p.m. on Friday, was the day of the Preparation on which the Passover lambs were sacrificed. This was the day of the Crucifixion. Therefore the Last Supper took place on the eve of the feast ; for the day of Preparation, while not regarded as the first day of the feast, nevertheless inaugurated it.

Nisan 15, i.e. 6 p.m. on Friday to 6 p.m. on Saturday, was the first day of the Passover on which the Passover meal took place. In this year the sabbath coincided with the first day of the Passover ; but according to Jewish custom a feast took precedence of the sabbath on such occasions.

Nisan 16, i.e. 6 p.m. on Saturday to 6 p.m. on Sunday, was the second day[1] of the Passover; it was also the first day of the week ; the day of the Resurrection, for it was the 'third day' from the Crucifixion.

This is the chronology according to the account given in the fourth Gospel. It is clear, logical, and consistent ; its minute and circumstantial detail is impressive and convincing.

Opposed to this account is that of the Synoptists, according to which the Last Supper took place during

---

[1] The 'second day' is, of course, not used here in its technical sense. The 'second day of festivals' was instituted by the Rabbis to obviate the possible ante-dating or post-dating of beginning a feast on the part of those living at a distance from Jerusalem.

or after the Passover meal which was held on the first day proper of the feast, viz. Nisan 15. This makes the Last Supper take place a whole day later than it does according to the fourth Gospel account. The difficulty which this involves will become very evident by considering the following table of Synoptic chronology:

Nisan 15, i.e. 6 p.m. on Friday to 6 p.m. on Saturday, was the first day of the Passover; on the Friday evening the Passover meal was eaten, during or after which the Eucharist was instituted. It was the Sabbath, which coincided this year with the first day of the Passover. It was during this day (i.e. the Saturday part of it) on which the Crucifixion took place (see Matt. xxvii. 1, *Now when morning was come*; cp. Mk. xv. 1; Lk. xxii. 66). On the evening of this day Christ was laid in the tomb (see Matt. xxvii. 57; Mk. xv. 42; Lk. xxiii. 50).

Nisan 16, i.e. 6 p.m. on Saturday to 6 p.m. on Sunday, was the second day of the Passover; but in Matt. xxvii. 62; Mk. xv. 42; Lk. xxiii. 54, this day is spoken of as *the day after the Preparation* (Matt.); *the day before the Sabbath* is added by St. Mark, and St. Luke implies the same.

Nisan 17, i.e. 6 p.m. on Sunday to 6 p.m. on Monday, being the third day from the Crucifixion ought logically to be the day of the Resurrection; but in Matt. xxviii. 1; Mk. xvi. 1; Lk. xxiv. 1, it is on the first day of the week that this takes place.

The difficulty of the Synoptic chronology in this matter is insuperable; and the question may well arise whether there is not behind the fourth Gospel a genuine historical tradition, which sometimes helps to supplement, sometimes even to correct, the Synoptic accounts.

A number of Jewish scholars, including such distinguished names as those of Abelson, Abrahams, Kohler, and Güdemann, have been greatly impressed with the genuinely Jewish character of the tradition behind the fourth Gospel; and the tendency of recent criticism has been, on the whole, to emphasize this. On the other hand, so great a scholar as Dalman, in his recently published book *Jesus-Jeshua*, where he devotes a large amount of space to the discussion of the character and details of the Last Supper, argues strongly in favour of the Synoptic accounts, and dismisses the representation of the fourth Gospel as unhistorical. He explains it as due to the Evangelist's desire to separate Jesus from Jewish observance, and to emphasize the symbolism of the Passion. It need scarcely be said that Dr. Dalman's discussion is set forth with a wealth of learning and scholarship which only he could command. Nevertheless, we confess that we are not convinced. His attempt to explain some of the difficulties inherent in the Synoptic accounts seems to us sometimes to savour of special pleading. But however this may be, Dr. Dalman does believe that the Last Supper was a Paschal meal, celebrated in an upper room on Nisan 15 with the elaboration appropriate to such a festive occasion within the holy city; and we do not wish to minimize the importance of this fact. But it seems to us that a number of considerations converge in favour of the Johannine narrative.

(*b*) The ritual details of the Passover meal are well known.[1] Among these was the drinking at certain

---

[1] An exceedingly good account will be found in Kingsbury's *Spiritual Sacrifice and Holy Communion*, pp. 139–53 (1900). For all details of the observances during the Passover meal see the Mishnah, *Pesachim* x. 1–9.

specified times during the meal, of four cups of wine, signifying, according to tradition, joy for the fourfold benefits granted to the Israelites by the delivery from the Egyptian bondage, viz. Freedom, Release, Redemption, Election (based on Exod. vi. 6, 7). It was necessary for each person present to have his own cup for this purpose. Now in the Synoptic Gospels (the fourth makes no reference at all to the subject) only one cup is mentioned; and all present drink from the one cup. Clearly this does not agree with the idea of the Last Supper having been a Passover meal. Moreover, in connexion with the cup, it is noticeable that there is not unanimity in the records concerning the question *when* it was partaken of. In Matthew and Mark it comes *after* the bread, while in Luke it comes *before* this ;[1] for the second mention of the cup, in Lk. xxii. 20, is not an original part of the text; this has been amply shown by a review of all the textual evidence given by Sanday in Hastings' *Dictionary of the Bible*, ii. 636. It is also somewhat striking that St. Paul is not consistent on this matter, for while in 1 Cor. xi. 23–27 he mentions the bread first and then the cup, in 1 Cor. x. 16, 21 he twice pointedly mentions the cup first and then the bread.

These last two points are, it is granted, not decisive; but it can hardly be denied that inasmuch as they seem to manifest some divergence from the well authenticated custom and procedure at the Passover meal, they raise the question whether it really was a Passover meal during which, or after which, the Eucharist was instituted.

(*c*) But another point, which is sometimes overlooked, and which cannot well be explained away, is

---

[1] This is also the case in the text of Cod. D.

that the Passover meal proper comes *after* the ritual blessing of the cup and the bread and their distribution; whereas, as we have already seen, the Gospel accounts make it perfectly clear that the meal which was being partaken of *preceded* the more solemn ceremony. This is an important consideration which will come before us again.

(*d*) Then there is another point worth mentioning. In Lk. xxii. 19 Christ says : *This do in remembrance of me* ; and St. Paul, quoting our Lord's words, says in 1 Cor. xii. 25 : *Do this, as often as ye drink it, in remembrance of me.* If it was the Passover meal during which these words were uttered, the most natural inference which Christ's hearers would draw would be that He was referring to the Passover cup ; but inasmuch as the Passover feast took place annually, the remembrance would, in that case, only be once a year. But, as we know from Acts xx. 7 and from other sources, it was from the very beginning the use of the Church to make this remembrance on every first day of the week.

(*e*) And lastly, if, as the Synoptists record, it was the Passover meal after which Christ went out and was betrayed, it would mean, as we have already seen, that the Crucifixion took place during the feast. But this, as well as the carrying of arms (Mk. xiv. 47 ; Lk. xxii. 38), the trial (Mk. xv. 1 ff., and the parallel passages), and the buying of spices (Mk. xvi. 1 ; Lk. xxiii. 56, xxiv. 1), are all unthinkable during the feast ; for all come under the category of work, and this was strictly forbidden by Jewish law during a feast. It is conceivable that the realization of this accounts for the insertion of the words ' because it was the Preparation,

that is, the day before the Sabbath', in Mk. xv. 42, ·
although at variance with what is said in xiv. 12
onwards. On the other hand, this difficulty does not
arise if we follow the record of the fourth Gospel,
according to which all these events occurred either
before or on the day of Preparation, i. e. before the
official beginning of the feast.

This discussion has taken us somewhat far afield;
and before we proceed it may be worth while to sum
up quite briefly what has been, so far, said :

Before the institution of the Eucharist took place,
a meal had been partaken of; the institution, therefore,
took place either during, or at the conclusion of, this
meal; the accounts point to the latter, since the going
forth occurs immediately after the institution; though
the words 'as they were eating' might imply that it
was during the meal.

When it was inquired what kind of a meal this was,
cogent reasons were given to show that it was not,
as is usually held, a Passover meal. Those reasons
were :

(1) The chronological discrepancy between the
Synoptic accounts and that of the fourth Gospel;

(2) The mention of one cup only, partaken of by
all, instead of each person present using his own cup
as at the Passover feast; and the uncertainty of the
records as to the order of the cup and the bread ;

(3) The fact that the meal *preceded* the blessing of
the cup and the bread, whereas the Passover meal
proper comes after this;

(4) The fact that the memorial at the Passover feast
would be annual, whereas from the very beginning the
memorial was weekly; and

(5) The further fact that if it had been the Passover meal it would have meant that the feast had already begun before the betrayal and the events recorded in connexion with the Crucifixion ; this would have been such an infraction of the Law forbidding work during the feast as to be incredible.

The cumulative effects of these arguments cannot be ignored. The different attempts which have been made to answer them have not solved the ̇difficulty. We must frankly face the fact that either the Synoptists are right, or the fourth Gospel ; they cannot possibly both be right according to the form of their respective accounts as we now have them.

If we accept the Synoptic accounts of the meal which is represented as a Passover meal we are confronted with difficulties which are found to be insuperable. On the other hand, if we accept the fourth Gospel account we must explain what the meal was, if it was not a Passover meal. And this is what we shall now proceed to do.

The theory which we shall advocate is, in the main, not new ; it has been put forth by several scholars, each of whom, so far as the present writer knows, reached his conclusion quite independently of the others.[1]   But there were some flaws in the argument.[2]

---

[1] Drews, in Hauck-Herzog's *Real-Encycl.* . . . , v. 563 ; Spitta, *Zur Geschichte und Litteratur des Urchristentums*, pp. 24 ff. (1893) ; Foxley, in the *Contemporary Review* (February 1899) ; Box, in the *Journal of Theological Studies*, iii, pp. 563 ff. (1902), and Burkitt, xvii, pp. 291 ff. (1916).

[2] Lambert, in the *Journal of Theological Studies*, iv, pp. 184 ff., and Blakiston, pp. 548 ff. (1903). See also Chwolson, *Das letzte Passamahl Christi und der Tag seines Todes* (1892) ; Srawley, *The Early History of the Liturgy*, pp. 6 ff. (1913) ; and Dalman's book referred to above.

We believe now, however, that in the light of some new evidence, we shall be able to present the theory in a more convincing form, and with its former weak points strengthened.

III

Among the Jews, some time after the Exile, but exactly when cannot be decided—at any rate well within pre-Christian times—it was the custom early on (what we should call) Friday afternoons for friends to meet together in the house of one of them and partake of a social meal. There was a distinctly religious atmosphere about these gatherings; religious topics were of paramount interest to the Jews, hence the subjects of conversation on these occasions were of a religious character.

These weekly gatherings were arranged by small groups or societies of friends. Such societies were called *Chabûrôth*[1] (sing. *Chabûrah*) from the word *Chabēr*, a 'comrade', 'companion', or 'friend'. The social, quasi-religious meal began fairly early in the afternoon, and was drawn out by conversation and discussion of religious questions until dusk. Then the meal was interrupted because the Sabbath was about to commence. He who presided at the table took a cup of wine and said a benediction over it for what was called the 'sanctification of the day' (*Kedūshath ha-yôm*).[2]

Elbogen says that 'on ordinary days it was customary in aristocratic circles to partake of the meal at the ninth

---

[1] These *Chabûrôth* existed for other purposes as well; while the members met, in the first instance, for partaking of a social meal, their *raison d'être* was to perform acts of piety and love, as indeed is implied by the word *Chabûrah*. See on this further below, pp. 172 ff.

[2] See Elbogen, *Op. cit.*, pp. 107, 111.

hour (*Pes.* 107 *b*) ; on Fridays, however, it was post-
poned by all classes to night-time (*Tos. Ber.* v. 3).'
This was, according to Rabbi Meir (second century A.D.),
the latest limit; the rule, as a matter of fact, was to
begin the meal earlier; for as it marked the actual
beginning of the Sabbath observance, the earlier it
began the more meritorious was it considered to be
(*Pes.* 105 *b*).   As late as the Tannaitic period there is
no doubt that the meal began during the daylight
(*Tos. Ber.* v. 2 ; cp. also *Pes.* 100 *a*, 102 *a*).   In these
last two passages it is said that darkness supervened
' during the meal', and that the Sabbath, which then
began, was greeted by a blessing over the cup (i.e. the
Kiddûsh cup, see below).   The custom was for the wine
to be served after some food had been partaken of.[1]
On this point both the house of Shammai and the
house of Hillel were in agreement (*Pes.* 114 *a*).   As
soon as the wine was brought a grace was said
(ברכת המזון), and there followed immediately the
prayer for the sanctification of the day (*Tos. Ber.*
v. 4).[2]

It is true that the *dictum* of a second century Rabbi
(R. Judah) is cited in *Tos. Ber.* v. 1 to the effect that
' a man does not eat on the eve of the Sabbath from
the afternoon and onwards, so that he may enter on
the Sabbath with desire'.   In other words this Rabbi

---

[1] At the Passover meal it was different, because of the four cups ;
see Baneth, *Der Sederabend*, p. 16.

[2] J. Lewy, 'Ein Vortrag über das Ritual des Pesach-Abends', in
Beilage zum Jahresbericht des Jüd. Theol. Seminars in Breslau, pp. 11 ff.
(1904).   Elbogen, 'Eingang und Ausgang des Sabbats nach tal-
mudischen Quellen', in *Festschrift zu Israel Lewy's* 70. *Geburtstag*,
pp. 179 ff. (1911); cp. also Rosenthal in Graetz, *Geschichte der
Juden* . . ., iv, pp. 469 ff. (4th ed., 1908).

deprecated any Friday afternoon meal at all. But his ruling was opposed by another authority, R. Jose ben Chalafta, a contemporary, who laid down the rule obviously justifying the older custom, that 'A man continues to eat [on Friday afternoon] until the time that it is getting dark'. All the evidence points to this custom having been specifically Palestinian in its origin, a fact which witnesses to its antiquity.

It is important to bear in mind that this social, quasi-religious meal, together with the subsequent ceremony of the 'sanctification of the day', took place in private houses, and had originally nothing to do either with the Temple, or, later, with the Synagogue worship.[1] In early post-Christian times both were transferred to the Synagogue; and eventually the meal itself was given up and only the ceremony of the sanctification of the Sabbath was retained. In still later times (and this is the practice at the present day), while the sanctification ceremony continued to be a liturgical one in the Synagogue, both it and the social meal reverted to their original place in the home; *but with this notable difference*, that whereas originally the meal preceded the sanctification ceremony, now

---

[1] The custom of ushering in the Sabbath during a meal in private houses continued certainly until the period of the Amoraim; there is evidence that at the beginning of this period the ushering in of the Sabbath took place in the Synagogue (*Jer. Pes.* x. 2; *Jer. Ber.* viii. 1). So far as Palestine is concerned all the evidence shows that the meal took place in the house. Not until the time of the Babylonian Amoraim, Rab, and Samuel is there any mention of its taking place in the Synagogue (*Pes.* 100 *b*).

'At these meals each member of the *Chabûrah* brought some food some time before the Sabbath (so as not to profane it) to the particular house in which the meal was about to be held' (Geiger, *Urschrift und Uebersetzungen der Bibel* ..., p. 124 [1857]).

the order was reversed, and the sanctification ceremony preceded the meal.

But to return; in the earliest references to this 'sanctification of the day' ceremony, although the benediction over the cup is spoken of, its distribution is not mentioned, nor is there any mention of the bread;[1] but this non-mention of the details of what was an extremely familiar ceremony will not cause surprise. But when both the meal and the sanctification ceremony are first mentioned as having been transferred to the Synagogue, the cup and the bread are both spoken of, as well as the blessing pronounced over each. The ceremony is then known by the name of *Kiddûsh*, which is simply an intensive form of the earlier name *Kĕdûshah*, 'Sanctification', i.e. of the Sabbath.

As an illustration of this custom in its *original* form mention may be made of an incident in the *Tosephta*[2] to the Mishnah tractate *Berakhôth* (v. 1). In reference to the Friday afternoon social and quasi-religious meal Rabbi Jose,[3] who lived during the middle of the second century A.D., is reported as saying that it is customary to partake of it until it is getting dark, i.e. until the Sabbath is drawing on (about 6 p.m.); the passage continues: 'An incident (is related) of Rabban Simeon ben Gamaliel and R. Judah and R. Jose, that they were reclining at the meal in Accho, and the holy day [i.e. the Sabbath] drew on. Rabban Simeon ben

---

[1] The blessing over the bread would already have been pronounced at the beginning of the meal.

[2] I.e. 'addition' or 'supplement' to the Mishnah proper, see *SLRJ*, pp. 108 ff.

[3] I.e. Jose ben Chalaphta, not to be confused with Jose the Galilaean, who lived a little earlier.

Gamaliel said to R. Jose, " Let us leave off [our meal] for the Sabbath " . . .'; then there follows a reference to the cup over which the sanctification of the day is said.[1] The passage is noteworthy as showing that originally *the meal came first*, then the sanctification ceremony.

And now we have a further and important fact to note regarding this matter. This meal, and the sanctification ceremony which followed, ushered in not only the weekly Sabbath, but also took place on the eve of the great festivals ; not that the mention of the Sabbath was omitted on such occasions ; as the holy day *par excellence* it was remembered when other holy days were ushered in ; both the Sabbath and the festival were commemorated. So that when, later, the sanctification ceremony was transferred to the Synagogue and received the name of *Kiddûsh*, each festival had its special *Kiddûsh*, and this obtains at the present day ; though, excepting for a reference to the feast, the words, together with the sanctification ceremony were, and are, much the same as for the weekly Sabbath ; so that the importance of the Sabbath and of its teaching was not lost sight of even when the first day of a festival coincided with it. We are, however, dealing with what obtained in pre-Christian times ; and the important difference between them and subsequent times was that the social meal came first, and then the sanctification ceremony. This consisted of the commemoration of the institution of the Sabbath, the blessing over the cup and its partaking of by all; then the memorial of redemption from the Egyptian bondage, followed by the blessing over the bread and its distribution.

[1] See Lukyn Williams's handy translation, p 57 (1921).

Now the suggestion that is here offered is as follows :

The circle of friends formed by Christ and the Apostles constituted a *Chabûrah.* According to John xv. 14 our Lord refers to this in the words, *Ye are my friends, if ye do the things which I command you.* They met, as they had doubtless done many a time before, for the usual weekly social meal. It was on a Thursday instead of a Friday on this particular occasion for reasons which will be explained presently. After the usual grace had been said the social meal began. The conversation, as always, turned upon religious subjects ; and, as we know, there were reasons why on this occasion they should have been of a specially solemn character. We may well believe that in their essence the subjects spoken of are preserved in John xiv–xvi ; certainly the points of contact in both thought and word between these chapters and the text of *Kiddûsh* are sufficiently striking. After the meal had continued for some time it began to draw towards dusk, and while they were still sitting at meat, He who presided at the table did as all present expected He would do ; He began the ceremony of sanctification ; and as it was the eve of the Passover feast, it took the usual form of the combined commemoration of the Sabbath and the redemption from the Egyptian bondage, i.e. Passover *Kiddûsh.* He took the cup, and said the usual blessing over it, but now gave it a new meaning. The cup was then passed round, and all partook of it. And the same with the bread. The circle of friends were commanded to do this in remembrance of Him.

Following the chronology of the fourth Gospel, the sanctification ceremony, which would have been technically known as ' Passover *Kiddûsh* ', took place on

Nisan 14, i. e. 6 p. m. on Thursday to 6 p. m. on Friday.
That means that on the Thursday afternoon (according
to Jewish reckoning, Nisan 13) they met together for
the social meal, in the way already described, until
the approach of Nisan 14, i.e. 6 p. m. on the same day
(according to our reckoning), when Passover *Kiddûsh*
was said, and the institution of the Eucharist took
place.

If, then, we identify the meal at which Christ and
His disciples were sitting with the weekly social meal
already alluded to, and if we identify the blessing of
the cup and the bread with the sanctification ceremony
known as ' Passover *Kiddûsh* ', all the difficulties, with
one notable exception (to be referred to presently)
disappear ; viz. :

i. In all the accounts, as we have seen, a meal was
taking place before the ceremony of the institution of
the Eucharist was celebrated.

ii. Since the Passover *Kiddûsh* took place on
Nisan 14, which was absolutely necessary in this
year, as will be shown presently, the difficulty of
what would have been regarded as a desecration of
the Feast is eliminated, namely, the Crucifixion itself,
the carrying of arms, the trial, and the buying of
spices ; for all these, occurring on Nisan 14, took
place, not during the actual Feast, but on the day
of Preparation.

iii. In the Synoptic accounts only one cup is spoken
of, which is partaken of by all ; they agree herein with
the custom at *Kiddûsh*.

iv. The uncertainty of the records as to the order
of reception is decided in favour of the cup being
received first.

v. The weekly celebration of the Eucharist accords with the weekly celebration of the *Kiddûsh*.

When all the facts are taken into consideration it must be allowed that there is something to be said for this theory. The antiquity both of the social meal and of *Kiddûsh* is not questioned. With regard to the latter, its text, as we have seen, is practically identical in all the ancient rituals; and when a liturgical piece can boast such purity of text it is a proof that it rests on sound tradition. And this fact has a special interest and importance for us, because we are enabled to say, if not exactly, yet very approximately, what the actual words were which Christ uttered over the cup and the bread; over the cup: 'Blessed art Thou, O Lord our God, Eternal King, who createst the fruit of the vine,' and over the bread: 'Blessed art Thou, O Lord our God, who bringest forth bread from the earth.' The words in each case are based on Scripture, viz. Ps. civ. 15.

What is striking is the extreme simplicity and shortness of the words in each case. The grace before meals was much longer; and though, in all probability, adapted in early forms of Christian worship before and after communion, must be regarded as quite distinct from the words uttered over the cup and the bread.

IV

There are some objections which will have suggested themselves in what has been said. These must be briefly dealt with.

i. It was pointed out that the social meal which preceded the sanctification ceremony took place on *Friday* afternoons, and that it was broken off at the approach of the Sabbath for the purpose of celebrating *Kiddûsh* (the sanctification ceremony). But, as we saw, the fourth Gospel makes it quite clear that it was on the *Thursday* afternoon that the meal took place. How does our theory square with this?

The answer is that in this year the Sabbath day coincided with the first day of the Passover Feast; on such occasions, according to ancient Jewish law, the Feast superseded the Sabbath.[1] The weekly social meal could not take place on the usual Friday afternoon, because the sacrificing of the Passover lambs was taking place in the Temple then; and the ordinary Sabbath *Kiddûsh* could not take place at 6 p.m. on Friday because the Passover meal was celebrated at this time in the year in question. Therefore the weekly social meal had to be held on the Thursday afternoon. At 6 p.m. on that Thursday began the day of Preparation, and Passover *Kiddûsh* was therefore said. It inaugurated the Feast; for although the day of Preparation was not regarded as the official first day of the Feast, yet, as being the day on which the Passover lambs were sacrificed (cp. Exod. xii. 2, 6), it was, in a very real sense, the introduction of the Feast.

ii. The second objection is a more serious one. How are we to account for the fact that, however faulty the chronology of the Synoptic accounts may be, they do, nevertheless, make the Passover meal that during or after which the Eucharist was instituted?

A good deal turns here on the fact that, according to the theory suggested (which is based on the evidence of the fourth Gospel), the Last Supper took place on the eve of the Day of Preparation, which means that

[1] See, for example, *Pesachim* vi. 1 ff.

the form of *Kiddûsh* said after the social meal was the Passover *Kiddûsh*,[1] in which the following occurs :

' Blessed art Thou, O Lord our God, Eternal King, who hast chosen us from all peoples, and exalted us above all tongues, and sanctified us by Thy commandments. And Thou hast given us in love, O Lord our God, appointed times for gladness, festivals and seasons for joy ; this day of the Feast of Un-leavened Bread, the season of our Freedom.'

This would create what one might describe as a Passover atmosphere, which would be indelibly im-pressed upon the minds of the disciples. This would be further emphasized by the fact that the Crucifixion took place on the day on which the Passover lambs were sacrificed. That day of Preparation, though not officially the first day of the Feast, would in the nature of things represent in the popular mind the actual beginning of it.

Then, further, *Kiddûsh*, *whenever* it was said, made mention of the holy day, the Sabbath, which was thought of as a ' memorial of the Creation', and as ' in remembrance of the departure out of Egypt', always conceived and spoken of as an act of divine redemp-tion.[2]

This, being all so familiar to the disciples and to the generation of Jewish-Christians that followed, was it

[1] The wording of this in the present Jewish Prayer-Book is practically identical with that of the oldest rites, thus proving its great antiquity ; see further, Abrahams, *Op. cit.*, p. cxciv.

[2] Cp. the words : ' From Egypt Thou didst redeem us, O Lord our God ', which occur in the prayer called *Gĕullah* (' Redemption '). This is one of the most ancient prayers of the Synagogue, and there are good grounds for believing that, in its original form, it belonged to the Temple Liturgy (see Zunz, *Op. cit.*, pp. 383 ff. ; Abrahams, *Op. cit.*, pp. lv ff. ; Elbogen, *Op. cit.*, pp. 23 ff.).

not the most natural thing in the world that they, in thinking of the sacrifice of Christ, and of His redemptive work, and of the memorial of Him, should have connected all these with the Passover, a great national institution, second only in importance to the Feast of Tabernacles, and have thought of the Last Supper as a Passover meal rather than of its connexion with *Kiddûsh*?

In this case it could justly be said that the Synoptic accounts reflect the popular conception, which in its essence was perfectly right, though chronologically inaccurate; while the fourth Gospel, written by one with more intimate knowledge, gives the more strictly accurate account.

iii. Once more, it may be objected that the whole setting of the accounts of the meal and the Institution in the Gospels suggest that the Supper took place after sunset, when night had supervened, which would preclude the possibility of a meal having been begun in the afternoon. It may be pointed out, however, that in the reconstruction set forth above, though the meal began in the afternoon it was prolonged till dusk and sunset. As twilight in the east is of very short duration, darkness quickly sets in; and the events which followed after the Supper would naturally have taken place when night had begun and it was darkness (cp. Jn. xiii. 30). We assume that before Judas took his departure the Institution had taken place, and that his exit followed immediately after. This entirely fits the Johannine narrative in Jn. xiii. Verse 31 begins: 'When therefore he was gone out, Jesus saith, Now is the Son of Man glorified, and God is glorified in him . . .'; in verse 33 Christ continues: '. . . whither I go

ye cannot come . . .'; then in verses 34, 35 : 'A new
commandment I give unto you, that ye love one
another; even as I have loved you, that ye also love
one another. By this shall all men know that ye are
my disciples, if ye have love one to another.' All
these words point back, it would seem, most naturally
to the Institution which has already taken place,
the significance of which they illuminate ; the solemn
partaking of the bread and wine was a bond of love
and union between the Master and His disciples. The
discourses which follow (chaps. xiv–xvii), which are
predominantly eucharistic in character, and which,
according to our view, are a summary (together with
chap. vi) of Christ's eucharistic teaching, possibly
spoken on more than one occasion, come naturally in
the Johannine narrative at this point. On the occasion
of the Last Supper Christ may have delivered a final
discourse of this kind, the substance of which is
embodied in these chapters. But it is not necessary
to suppose that the chapters as a whole represent a
long discourse uttered at this point. It is perhaps
more reasonable to hold that these chapters, which
some scholars regard as misplaced or interpolated,
reflect conversations which had taken place during the
meal itself. If this be so, the next point in the historical sequence is reached in chap. xviii. 1 : 'When
Jesus had spoken these words . . .', i.e. the words
contained in xiii. 36–38 : '. . . Jesus said, Whither I
go thou canst not follow me now. . . . Jesus answereth,
Wilt thou lay down thy life for me ? Verily, verily,
I say unto thee, The cock shall not crow, till thou hast
denied me thrice.'

A further objection may be raised in connexion with
the phrase used by the Synoptists at the beginning of

their account of the Last Supper : 'Now when even was come' (ὀψίας δὲ γενομένης, Matt. xxvi. 20 ; Mk. xiv. 17). Does this not imply that the meal was begun after dark ? The answer to this question is certainly in the negative. 'Οψία does not necessarily mean anything more than the later afternoon, and gives room for a substantial period before sunset.[1]

It may, therefore, be asserted that the reconstruction suggested above is not incompatible with the salient features of the Synoptic tradition.

---

[1] See Grim-Thayer, s.v.

FURTHER ARGUMENTS IN SUPPORT OF THE THEORY ADVOCATED IN THE PRECEDING CHAPTER

In the preceding chapter some reasons have been given for the contention that it was not a Passover meal at which the Eucharist was instituted. We reserve for a separate chapter some further considerations in favour of the theory advocated. Had these been dealt with in the previous chapter the consequent digressions would have interrupted the course of the argument, hence their treatment here. But we wish to emphasize the fact that these considerations are in no wise unimportant for the general argument; in forming a final judgement our readers will, we hope, carefully weigh them.

I

We deal first with some New Testament passages.

(*a*) In the Synoptic Gospels there are, on the one hand, certain features which point indubitably to a Passover meal as that during which, or at the conclusion of which, the Last Supper was instituted. These are so familiar that it will not be necessary to indicate them. On the other hand, there are some features which do not in themselves suggest a Paschal meal. These are worth a little examination.

In Matt. xxvi. 17; Mk. xiv. 12; Lk. xxii. 8 the meal which is being partaken of is definitely referred to as a Passover meal. But it is worth noting that in the accounts of the Supper itself it is not spoken of as that of the Passover. Indeed, one passage can be justifiably interpreted as excluding this, though we recognize, of course, that a different interpretation can, perhaps as justifiably, be given. The passage is Lk. xx. 15, 16, which we venture to paraphrase thus: 'Greatly did I desire to eat this passover, i. e. to celebrate this feast, with you before I suffer; but it is not to be, for I say unto you, I will not eat it, until it be fulfilled in the Kingdom of God.'[1] It must be allowed that this definite assertion on the part of Christ that He will not partake of the feast, justifies the contention that the words, 'with desire did I desire' ($\dot{\epsilon}\pi\epsilon\theta\acute{v}\mu\eta\sigma\alpha$), express an unfulfilled wish.[2] The words are interpreted in an opposite sense by the late Dr. Buchanan Gray in a passage which, from another point of view, points to a strange omission in the Synoptic accounts; he says: 'Most remarkable is the fact that neither Mark nor Matthew refers to the central feature of the Jewish Passover meal, viz. the roasted Paschal flesh. This is, according to Jewish usage, implied, not to say immediately referred to, in the words, "I have greatly desired to eat this Passover with you". If Matthew and Mark represent the common basis of the Synoptic tradition then in that basis the Paschal victim was not mentioned in the account of the Last Supper, and Luke's addition has the effect of giving greater emphasis to the view common to the Passion narratives

---

[1] Matt. xxvi. 5 is worth recalling here: 'But they said, Not during the feast, lest a tumult arise among the people.'

[2] We do not lay stress on the point, seeing the character and tendency of the document in which the following words occur, but it may be worth noting that in the *Gospel of the Ebionites*, quoted by Epiphanius (*Haer.* xxx. 22), the passage is rendered: 'I have not desired to eat this Passover flesh with you.'

of all three Gospels in their present form that the Last
Supper was a Passover.'¹ While unable to accept this
interpretation of Lk. xx. 15, 16, especially in view
of its context, we recognize the force of what is here
said about the silence regarding the central feature of
the Jewish Passover Meal.

(*b*) Another point mentioned by Dr. Gray is in
reference to the term used in the narratives for bread :
' This is always the general term ἄρτος, never ἄζυμα,
corresponding to the Hebrew *lechem* and *mazzôth* ; now
it is, on the one hand, certain that in Hebrew the
general includes the special term, that *mazzôth*, " un-
leavened bread ", could be called *lechem*, " bread " ; but,
on the other hand, to judge from uses in the Jewish
sources it was customary not to use the general, but
the special term in speaking of the Paschal meal ; at
the same time, it is not conclusive.' Nevertheless, we
cannot help feeling that it is remarkable that ἄζυμα is
not used here when we find all three Synoptists are
familiar with the term (Matt. xxvi. 17 ; Mk. xiv. 1, 12 ;
Lk. xxii. 1, 7) ; and, further, ἄρτος occurs over and over
again in connexion with ordinary meals, so that its use at
this meal would go to suggest that it was not a Paschal
meal.² Some words of Prof. Sanday's are apposite
in this connexion : ' We are reminded that the phrase
κλᾶν (κατακλᾶν) ἄρτον is repeatedly used of a solemn act
of our Lord independently of the Eucharist (Mk. vi. 41,
viii. 6, 19 ; Lk. xxiv. 30). We are reminded also of
the many instances in which attention is specially called
to the "blessing" (εὐλογεῖν or εὐχαριστεῖν) of food by our
Lord. They are the same words which are used in

¹ A communication kindly made to me by Dr. Theodore Robinson.
² Leavened bread could be eaten until midday of Nisan 14 (*Pes.* i. 4,
ii. 1 ff.) ; the Last Supper took place before this, as we have seen.

connexion with the sacramental bread and the sacramental cup. There is something in these facts which is not quite fully explained. There are *lacunae* in our knowledge which we would fain fill up if we could. The institution of the Eucharist appears to have connexions both backwards and forwards,—backwards with other meals which our Lord ate together with His disciples, forwards with those common meals which very early came into existence in the Apostolic Church. But the exact nature and method of these connexions our materials are not sufficient to make clear to us.'[1] Can we solve the difficulty in the light of the facts which have been brought forward?

(*c*) A further consideration which bears indirectly on our subject, and is, therefore, the more telling, is that the offering of the Sheaf of the Firstfruits (ἀπαρχή) was offered on the morning of Nisan 16,[2] at any rate according to the practice of the first century A.D., i.e. on the second day of the Feast of Passover. In 1 Cor. xv. 20 St. Paul says : ' But now hath Christ been raised from the dead, the firstfruits of them that are asleep ' (ἀπαρχὴ τῶν κεκοιμημένων). This would seem to imply clearly that St. Paul believed that the Crucifixion took place on Nisan 14, thus agreeing with the chronology of the fourth Gospel.[3] This being so, we are justified in taking the words of 1 Cor. v. 7 (' For our passover also hath been sacrificed, even Christ ') in the sense of a contrast ; the ordinary Passover Lamb had been sacrificed, according to the old dispensation, but we too have our Passover Lamb, who has likewise

---

[1] Hastings's *DB*, iii. 637.

[2] For details of the offering see Mishnah, *Menachôth* x. 1–4.

[3] My acknowledgements are due to Dr. Theodore Robinson, who drew my attention to this.

been sacrificed. And it is this thought of Christ as the Passover Lamb which leads St. Paul to continue the contrast by pointing to the difference between the leaven of malice and wickedness, and the unleavened bread of sincerity and truth. His words, 'wherefore let us keep the feast, not with old leaven . . .', show that he has not in mind a literal connexion between Christ and the Passover, otherwise he would not have spoken of keeping the feast with leaven.

(*d*) We pointed out in the preceding chapter that during the weekly quasi-religious meals, at one of which, according to our contention, the Last Supper was instituted, the subjects of conversation were usually of a more solemn or religious character; and we expressed our belief in the possibility that on this particular occasion the essence of the subjects spoken of may well have been preserved in John xiv–xvii. That on this occasion the chief speaker should have been our Lord was natural enough (but see xiii. 36–38; xiv. 5–10, 22, 23; xvi. 17, 18, 29, 30). We remarked, further, that the points of contact between these chapters and the text of *Kiddûsh* (in this case it was Passover-*Kiddûsh*) were striking; though it is not so much individual parallelisms of thought as the general development of the ideas contained in *Kiddûsh* which suggests that it formed the background and starting-point of much that these chapters contain. It will be of interest to illustrate this.

The outstanding thoughts of Passover-*Kiddûsh* may be briefly enumerated thus :[1]

(i) The finishing of the work of Creation, culminating in the divine hallowing of the Sabbath.

(ii) The words: ' Blessed art Thou, O Lord our

[1] For the full text see p. 81.

God, King of the Universe, who createst the fruit of the vine.'

(iii) The memorial of the departure from Egypt, in which there always centred the thought of redemption.

(iv) The election of Israel and its sanctification above all nations.

(v) The words: ' Blessed art Thou, O Lord our God, King of the Universe, who bringest forth bread from the earth.'

(vi) The thought of freedom, suggested by the Passover season.

(vii) The thought of joy which the Passover season brings.

Thus, apart from the mention of the Vine and the Bread, the main thoughts may be expressed by the words: Completion of work, Redemption, Election, Freedom, Joy.

The thought of the Vine is elaborated in xv. 1 ff., ' I am the true vine . . .'; cp. also verses 8, 16 ; and as the drinking of the *Kiddûsh*-cup was by far the more important part of the ceremony of *Kiddûsh*, the prominence given to the teaching on the vine is what we should expect. The mention of bread in xiii. 18 cannot be pressed.

As to the other thoughts, it is perhaps not fanciful to discern that of the completion of the work of Creation, contained in *Kiddûsh*, behind the assertion of the completion of the new creative work spoken of in xvii. 4, 5 : ' I glorified thee on the earth, having accomplished the work which thou hast given me to do. And now, O Father, glorify thou me with thine own self with the glory which I had with thee before the world was.' If

A a

these last words, as can hardly be doubted, contain an implicit reference to i. 1-3, then we must see in them an allusion to the creative power of the Word in the beginning—'All things were made by him . . .' (i. 3).

Again, as we have already pointed out, the deliverance from the Egyptian bondage is always indissolubly connected with the idea of redemption and all that this implies. With this thought, suggested by the words of *Kiddûsh*, in the minds of Christ's hearers, such words as the following must have had a deep significance for them : 'Ye believe in God, believe also in me. In my Father's house are many mansions ; if it were not so I would have told you : for I go to prepare a place for you' (xiv. 1, 2). The disciples were Jews, and believed in the divine act of redemption which the God of their fathers had accomplished in delivering them from the Egyptian bondage, and leading them to the promised land. Now they were bidden to believe in the Divine Son of God, who told them of another promised land.

The Election of Israel was a very familiar theme to all Jews, and it is pointedly referred to in *Kiddûsh*. This thought must assuredly have lain behind the words : 'I know whom I have chosen' (xiii. 18) ; 'Ye did not choose me, but I chose you' (xv. 16); 'Because ye are not of the world, but I chose you out of the world, therefore the world hateth you' (xv. 19).

The thought of Freedom, which Passover-*Kiddûsh* speaks of as connected with the feast, does not appear so obviously as the others, though it is implicit in such a passage as xv. 15 : 'No longer do I call you bond-servants, for the bond-servant knoweth not what his lord doeth : but I have called you friends ; for all things that I heard from my Father I have made known unto you.'

On the other hand, the thought of Joy which is likewise mentioned in Passover-*Kiddûsh*, appears several times in these chapters : ' These things have I spoken unto you, that my joy may be in you, and that your joy may be fulfilled ' (xv. 11) ; '. . . and your joy no one taketh away from you' (xvi. 22) ; '. . . these things I speak in the world, that they may have my joy fulfilled in themselves ' (xvii. 13).

This community of thought between *Kiddûsh* and much that occurs in these chapters—and it is probable that we have not exhausted the subject—is, then, a subsidiary argument in favour of the theory put forward in the preceding chapter.

II

Turning now from the New Testament, there are a few indications in some early Christian documents which go to support our thesis.

(*a*) The relevant passages of the *Didaché* occur in chaps. ix, x, xiv. In chap. ix we get the following account of the Eucharist :

' And concerning the thanksgiving ($\tau\hat{\eta}s$ $\epsilon\dot{v}\chi\alpha\rho\iota\sigma\tau\dot{\iota}\alpha s$) thus give thanks ($\epsilon\dot{v}\chi\alpha\rho\iota\sigma\tau\dot{\eta}\sigma\alpha\tau\epsilon$). First concerning the cup : " We give thanks to Thee, our Father, for the holy vine of David Thy servant, which Thou didst make known to us through Thy servant Jesus. To Thee be glory for ever." And concerning that which is broken ($\tau o\hat{v}$ $\kappa\lambda\dot{\alpha}\sigma\mu\alpha\tau os$) : " We give thanks to Thee, our Father, for the life and knowledge which Thou didst make known to us through Thy servant Jesus. To Thee be glory for ever." ' The words which follow form a prayer which does not strike one as having belonged to the words of thanksgiving. The phrase 'To Thee be glory for ever' seems in each case to conclude the actual words said over the cup and bread respectively.

What must immediately strike one here is that the cup is mentioned first, and then the bread. That is the order in the *Kiddûsh* ceremony.

In comparing the words said over the elements in *Kiddûsh* and the *Didaché* respectively, there is a strong suggestion that the latter has adapted the wording of the former to a Christian use : regarding the words said over the cup, the *Didaché* expression 'the holy vine' is based on 'the fruit of the vine' in *Kiddûsh*. The reference to David in the *Didaché* expresses the thoughts suggested by such phrases as 'the root of Jesse', 'the Son of David', which in both the Jewish and Christian Church were connected with the coming of the Messianic Kingdom, the thought of which must have been present at the eucharistic celebration when one recalls such passages as Matt. xxvi. 29 : 'But I say unto you, I will not drink henceforth of this fruit of the vine, until that day when I drink it new with you in my Father's kingdom', uttered immediately after the institution ; and 1 Cor. xi. 26 : 'For as often as ye eat this bread, and drink the cup, ye proclaim the Lord's death till he come' (cp. Jn. xxi. 22); we may note also at the end of the sections on the Eucharist in the *Didaché* the formula 'Maranatha, Amen'. See also chap. xvi of the *Didaché*.

The entire absence in the *Didaché* of all reference to the words 'This is my Body', 'This is my Blood' is to be explained, we are convinced, by the fact that this manual was 'written with a view to the practical needs of the congregation *as a whole*, not of its officers. Hence the section on the Eucharist supplies merely forms of thanksgiving for the use of the recipient, not a formula of consecration for the celebrant.   Further, as Dr. Charles Taylor has pointed out, its "meagreness", in many details, "is proof that the *Didaché* must have been supplemented by oral teaching ".'[1]   This oral teaching will, however, have been facilitated at the first by the fact that it had some points of attachment with the familiar phraseology of *Kiddûsh*.

One other point may be briefly referred to—it will come before us again in dealing with the *Agapé*; we saw in the last chapter that, according to all the accounts, the Eucharist was instituted after a meal had taken place.   In the *Didaché* (xiv. 1) we see that this custom was still preserved, though the meal was transferred to Sunday :

'On the Lord's Day of the Lord come together, break bread, and celebrate the Eucharist' (εὐχαρισ-τήσατε).   It is realized that there are differences of opinion as to whether 'breaking of bread' here refers to the *Agapé* or not; see further below, p. 198 f.

(*b*) We consider next some points in Justin Martyr's *First Apology*, i. 65–67 and in his *Dialogue with Trypho*, 41, 70, 117.   As far as can be gathered from the scattered notices in these two works, the content of the central Eucharistic Prayer consisted of two main parts :

(1) Praise and thanksgiving to God for the gifts of Creation and for the redemption of mankind ; and

(2) The commemoration (ἀνάμνησις) of Christ's commandment, 'This do in remembrance of Me'.   The words of consecration are not given, but they seem to be referred to when Justin says (*Apol.* i. 66) : '. . . we

---

[1] Box, in the *Journal of Theological Studies*, iii. 367 f. (1902).

have been taught that the food for which thanks have been given *by the word of prayer which is from Him* (δι' εὐχῆς λόγου τοῦ παρ' αὐτοῦ) [1] . . . is the flesh and blood of that Jesus who was made flesh.'

In view of a further reference to be made to *Kiddûsh* in a moment, we would draw particular attention to the three dominant notes here : Creation, redemption, commemoration. Now in *Kiddûsh* before the benediction over the cup is said there is a reference to the Creation in the following words : ' And the heaven and the earth were finished and all their host. . . . And God blessed the seventh day, and He hallowed it, because He rested thereon from all His work which God had created and made.' Then, after the benediction over the cup, comes the following : ' Blessed art Thou, O Lord our God, King of the universe, who hast sanctified us by Thy commandments and hast taken pleasure in us, and in love and favour hast given us Thy holy Sabbath as an inheritance, a memorial of the Creation, that day being also the first day of the holy convocations, in remembrance of the departure from Egypt. . . . Blessed art Thou, O Lord, who hallowest the Sabbath.'

It is significant that in Justin's account of the Eucharistic Prayer the foremost notes (apart from the Sabbath) are *Creation* and *Commemoration*, just as in *Kiddûsh* ; that he makes no reference to the Sabbath is in the nature of things ; but thanksgiving for the gift of Creation and the redemption of mankind, followed by the *anamnesis*, the remembrance, does suggest an adaptation of the central thoughts of

---

[1] These words are interpreted differently by some scholars ; see Woolley, *Op. cit.*, p. 62 ; Srawley, *Op. cit.*, p. 35. Brightman, *Journal of Theological Studies*, i. 112, interprets as above.

Kiddûsh (apart from the Sabbath). There is also special significance in the remembrance of the departure from Egypt, for, as we have already seen, release from the Egyptian bondage was always thought of as an act of divine redemption. These parallel thoughts can scarcely be due to mere coincidence; rather they justify us in seeing in Justin's account the marks of the influence of *Kiddûsh*.

(*c*) A consideration of the two following passages from the *Dialogue with Trypho* make it clear that Justin cannot have believed that the institution of the Eucharist took place at the Passover meal. In 99 he says: 'In that day in which He was about to be crucified (τῇ ἡμέρᾳ ᾗπερ ἔμελλε σταυροῦσθαι) He took three of His disciples with Him to the Mount of Olives, as it was called . . .' In 111 he says: 'It is written that ye took Him and crucified Him on the day of the Passover' (ἐν τῇ ἡμέρᾳ τοῦ Πάσχα συνελάβετε αὐτόν . . .). But ἡ ἡμέρα τοῦ Πάσχα is Nisan 14; so that, according to Justin, the day on which Christ was crucified was the day on which they took Him in the garden of Gethsemane, i. e. on the Thursday after 6 p. m. It was the same day (i. e. Nisan 14, but on the part of it which we should call Friday) on which Christ was crucified. Therefore, according to Justin, it would appear that the Last Supper must have taken place on the day before this, Nisan 13, i. e. on the Thursday before 6 p. m.; and therefore the meal during or after which the Eucharist was instituted cannot have been the Passover meal.[1] It was the eve of the Sabbath,

[1] Possibly Justin's words are open to some ambiguity of meaning; whether he clearly realized himself the distinction between Nisan 14 and 15 is perhaps doubtful; but the interpretation suggested above is, on the whole, the most natural one.

and it is difficult to think of any other meal that it could have been than that to which reference has been made and which was followed by the *Kiddûsh* ceremony, on this occasion its Passover form, which inaugurated the Sabbath.

(*d*) Next, we have an interesting passage, belonging to about A. D. 165, which contains the words of Apollinarius, bishop of Hierapolis; it is worth giving in full:

Καὶ Ἀπολλινάριος δὲ ὁ ὁσιώτατος ἐπίσκοπος Ἱεραπόλεως τῆς Ἀσίας, ὁ ἐγγὺς τῶν ἀποστόλων χρόνων γεγονώς, ἐν τῷ περὶ τοῦ Πάσχα λόγῳ τὰ παραπλήσια ἐδίδαξε, λέγων οὕτως· Εἰσὶ τοίνυν οἳ δ᾽ ἄγνοιαν φιλονεικοῦσι περὶ τούτων, συγγνωστὸν πρᾶγμα πεπονθότες· ἄγνοια γὰρ οὐ κατηγορίαν ἀναδέχεται, ἀλλὰ διδαχῆς προσδεῖται· καὶ λέγουσιν ὅτι τῇ ιδ᾽ τὸ πρόβατον μετὰ τῶν μαθητῶν ἔφαγεν ὁ Κύριος, τῇ δὲ μεγάλῃ ἡμέρᾳ τῶν Ἀζύμων αὐτὸς ἔπαθεν, καὶ διηγοῦνται Ματθαῖον οὕτω λέγειν ὡς νενοήκασιν· ὅθεν ἀσύμφωνός τε νόμῳ ἡ νόησις αὐτῶν καὶ στασιάζειν δοκεῖ κατ᾽ αὐτοὺς τὰ Εὐαγγέλια.[1]

There was, thus, controversy at this time on the question as to whether Christ ate the Paschal lamb with His disciples on Nisan 14 and suffered on Nisan 15; also as to what the evidence of St. Matthew on the subject was. Apollinarius calls those who maintained that Christ ate the Passover on Nisan 14 and was crucified on Nisan 15 'ignorant' and 'quarrelsome'. This means, at any rate, that some, as late as A.D. 165, believed that the chronology of the fourth Gospel represented the true tradition.

Clement of Alexandria, a little later, held the same opinion; the passage in question is too long to quote, but will be found in the *Chron. Pasch.* (Migne, *PG* xcii,

---

[1] *Chronicon Paschale* (Dindorf, in Migne, *PG* xcii, col. 80).

col. 81). On the subject of the Quartodeciman controversy Brightman's admirable article in the *Journal
of Theological Studies* for April 1924 (pp. 254–270)
should be consulted.

These, then, are the further considerations which
should be weighed in forming a conclusion on the
theory of the antecedents of the Eucharist advocated
in the preceding chapter.

VIII

THE ORIGIN OF THE AGAPÉ

·I

APART from the Gospels, the first direct and indisputable evidence we have of a common meal in connexion with the Eucharist is in 1 Cor. xi. 20–34. The words in verse 20, 'When therefore ye assemble yourselves together', imply an habitual custom ; so that we are justified in believing that from the very beginning there was a common meal in connexion with the Eucharist. The word used for the meal (δεῖπνον), while not necessarily implying an evening meal, would most naturally be understood in that sense. Verses 20, 21, taken in their obvious meaning, show that the meal was first partaken of, and was followed by the Eucharist. Lightfoot [1] says: 'In the Apostolic age the eucharist formed part of the agapé. The original form of the Lord's Supper, as it was first instituted by Christ, was thus in a manner kept up. This appears from 1 Cor. xi. 17 sq. (cp. Acts xx. 7), from which passage we infer that the celebration of the eucharist came, as it naturally would, at a late stage in the entertainment.' St. Paul implies, furthermore, that this order was based on Christ's example : 'In like manner also the cup, *after supper*' (μετὰ τὸ δειπνῆσαι, verse 25).

This is the earliest written evidence, and if in the light of it we read Acts ii. 42, 44–46 (which, though it

---

[1] *Op. cit.*, vol. ii, sect. i, p. 313.

gives later documentary evidence, reflects the custom
of a still earlier time), we may reasonably assume that
'the breaking of bread' in verse 42, while referring to
the Eucharist, implies the preceding meal as a matter
of course. In verse 46 both the Eucharist and the
meal seem to be indicated.

Again, in Acts xx. 7–12 we have a passage which
must be read in the light both of 1 Cor. xi, 20–34 and
the account of the Last Supper in the Gospels. 'And
upon the first day of the week, when we were gathered
together to break bread'; here, while the Eucharist is
clearly meant, this 'breaking of bread' includes the
preceding meal. This is further suggested by the
protracted time during which the meeting lasted. At
the Last Supper, as pointed out in an earlier chapter,
the meal which preceded the actual institution was
drawn out, in all probability, by conversation and by
Christ's discourse of which a summary is contained (as
was suggested) in Jn. xiv–xvi. This seems to have
been the procedure as recounted in the passage before
us; they meet together to break bread, which began
with a common meal; during the meal St. Paul 'discourses with them'; and finally the Eucharist is
celebrated (verse 11). It is not fanciful, we think,
to distinguish between the words 'to break bread' in
verse 7, and 'And when he . . . had broken *the*
bread'; in Acts ii. 42 the article certainly seems to
point to the term being a technical one meaning the
Eucharist. But the point may not be pressed because
in Acts ii. 46 the article is not used though 'breaking
of bread' presumably refers there to the Eucharist.[1]

So far, then, the evidence justifies the conclusion

[1] In Acts xxvii. 35 an ordinary meal is spoken of, and the article
is not used.

that in the earliest Christian times a meal was partaken of in connexion with the Eucharist, and that it preceded the Eucharist ; in other words, the procedure at the institution of the Eucharist is followed.

But this meal is nowhere, in the passages referred to, spoken of as the *Agapé*. The first mention of the word occurs in Jude 12 : ' These are they who are hidden rocks in your love-feasts (ἐν ταῖς ἀγάπαις ὑμῶν) when they feast with you ' ; and in 2 Pet. ii. 13 : ' . . . spots and blemishes, revelling in their love-feasts (ἐν ταῖς ἀγάπαις[1] αὐτῶν) while they feast with you.' In neither of these passages is there any hint of the *Agapé* being connected with the Eucharist ; they only witness to the existence of the meal and its name, without specifying on what occasions it was held. It is only in the light of later evidence that it may be regarded as probable that these love-feasts were connected with the Eucharist. In both these passages the way in which they are referred to shows that they were well known ; the term *Agapé* is used in a technical sense although this is its first occurrence in biblical literature.

II

The earliest post-biblical evidence on the subject occurs in Ignatius' *Ep. to the Smyrnaeans*, viii. 2 : ' It is not lawful either to baptize or to hold a love-feast (ἀγάπην ποιεῖν) without a bishop.' In the preceding verse it is said : ' Let that be accounted a valid Eucharist which is under the bishop, or one whom he appoints.' At first sight this looks as though the

---

[1] We assume that this is the correct reading, but there is good manuscript authority for ἀπάταις.

Agapé had been separated from the Eucharist; but there is great point in what Lightfoot says:

' The words οὔτε βαπτίζειν οὔτε ἀγάπην ποιεῖν seem to describe the two most important functions in which the bishop could bear a part, so that the ἀγάπη must include the eucharist.   Indeed there would be an incongruity in this juxtaposition unless the other great sacrament were intended . . .   Nor would the omission of the eucharist be intelligible.   Pearson indeed urges " de eucharistia ante locutus est "; but this fact would not dispense with the mention here, where it is imperatively demanded ' (*Op. cit.*, II. i, pp. 313 ff.).

Ignatius does not, it is true, ever use *Agapé* as synonymous with the Eucharist; but two passages are worth quoting in this connexion; *Ep. to the Trallians*, viii. 1 : ' Therefore do ye take upon yourselves meekness and be renewed in faith which is the flesh of the Lord, and in love which is the blood of Jesus Christ.' This last sentence at once suggests the thought of a connexion between the *Agapé* and the Eucharist; we do not mean that the words are intended to imply this; but when we get the two words ἀγάπη and αἷμα together in a sentence like this one cannot well help thinking of the closeness of the two rites.   The other passage is the *Ep. to the Romans*, vii. 3 : ' The bread of God do I desire, which is the flesh of Jesus Christ, who is of the seed of David; and the drink I desire is His blood which is love incorruptible.'   Here again we have the close proximity of αἷμα and ἀγάπη suggesting the thought of the connexion between the Eucharist and the *Agapé*.   Ignatius' evidence thus *points* to the connexion between the Eucharist and the common meal which he speaks of as the *Agapé*, though it cannot be said that his evidence is conclusive.

We come next to the *Didaché*. There are three passages which come into consideration. The first, chap. ix, refers to the Eucharist only :

'And concerning the Eucharist, thus celebrate the Eucharist (οὕτως εὐχαριστήσατε) : First concerning the cup, "We give thanks to Thee, our Father, for the holy vine of David Thy servant ; to Thee be glory for ever". And concerning the broken bread, "We give thanks to Thee, our Father, for the life and knowledge which Thou didst make known to us through Jesus Thy servant. To Thee be glory for ever." As this broken bread . . . [this is quoted above, p. 131]. But let none eat or drink of your Eucharist except those who have been baptized in the Lord's Name ; for concerning this also did the Lord say, "Give not that which is holy to the dogs".'

There is nothing here to suggest any reference to a meal ; it is only the central part of the Eucharistic service itself that the writer speaks of. The second passage is chap. x. This begins thus : 'But after ye are filled, thus celebrate the Eucharist (Μετὰ δὲ τὸ ἐμπλησθῆναι οὕτως εὐχαριστήσατε) : "We give thanks to Thee, Holy Father . . .".' Taking these words in their most natural sense it must be clear that two things are referred to. 'After ye are filled' must have reference to food which has been partaken of before the celebrating of the Eucharist; in which case the procedure follows that of the Gospel accounts of the Last Supper, and of Acts xx. 7–12 and 1 Cor. xi. 20 ff. A difficulty only arises if chaps. ix and x of the *Didaché* be supposed to belong together. But why should they ? The *Didaché* is not a consistent treatise in which the chapters follow in logical sequence ; they read for the most part like disconnected fragments, intended perhaps ultimately for a book of instruction.

If chap. x stood where chap. xiv does, which also treats of the Eucharist, there could scarcely be any question of 'after ye are filled' not referring to a preceding meal. Believing, then, that the chapters of the *Didaché*, as we now have it, are independent pieces not necessarily connected with one another, we regard chap. x as standing independently of chap. ix, in the same way that chap. xiv is also independent of it; and that, therefore, the evidence of chap. ix points to a meal preceding the Eucharist.

The third passage is chap. xiv : 'On the Lord's Day of the Lord, when ye are assembled, break bread and celebrate the Eucharist. . . .' This seems to bear out what, it is contended, is meant by the passage just considered. 'Break bread' and 'celebrate the Eucharist', while clearly distinguished, belong together; the former will then refer to the common meal which preceded the Eucharist. The term *Agapé* is not used in the *Didaché*; probably the writer was not acquainted with it; but the important thing is that he witnesses to a meal preceding the Eucharist, thus bearing out the New Testament evidence.

The evidence of Pliny's letter to Trajan is too indefinite to build much on; the only thing that seems certain is that the common meal had been separated from the Eucharist, owing very likely to Trajan's edict;[1] but this separation would not necessarily have been universal.

Neither Justin Martyr nor Irenaeus gives any information about the *Agapé*, excepting that the former shows that the *Agapé* had been separated from the Eucharist;[2]

---

[1] See further, Lightfoot, *Op. cit.*, i, pt. 2, pp. 51 ff., 386.
[2] See his *Apol.* i. 65, 67.

this would be between thirty and forty years after the persecution under Trajan.

Clement of Alexandria refers to love-feasts which he calls *Agapae*, but denounces the abuses which took place at them. In Alexandria in his day the *Agapé* was not separated from the Eucharist, whatever obtained elsewhere.[1]

Tertullian also speaks of abuses at the *Agapé*.[2] According to both these writers it is evident that the *Agapé* was separated from the Eucharist. This continued to be the case until the end of the seventh century, when the *Agapé* was finally abolished.

Thus, although our information regarding the *Agapé* and its relation to the Eucharist is not all that we could desire, the evidence as a whole justifies us in saying that from the beginning, up till towards the middle of the second century, the *Agapé* was connected with the Eucharist in the closest way, and that it was a common meal which preceded the Eucharist.

III

As to the origin of the *Agapé*, Bishop Maclean has summarized the various theories thus:

'Most writers have seen in the custom an endeavour to follow the precedent of the Last Supper, when the Eucharist was combined with a meal. It is also thought that the early Christians were copying the Jews, who had social meals, or the Greeks and Romans, who had clubs, of which banquets were a prominent feature. The origin of the *Agapé* has also been looked for in the funeral feasts which were common among both Jews and Gentiles. Or it has been thought to have

---

[1] *Paedag.* ii. 1. 12.

[2] *De Jejuniis* xvii (*PL* ii, col. 1029); this was while he was still a Montanist.

arisen simply from the early communism of the Apostolic Church (Acts iv. 32).'[1]

This last theory sounds convincing ; but the lack of positive evidence makes it difficult either to maintain or to refute it ; and unless one had something *more* convincing to put in its place it might well stand. But the present writer believes that he has something more convincing to offer.

As to the *Agapé* having been a funeral banquet, a recent writer, Leclercq, in quoting 1 Cor. xi. 26 ('For as often as ye eat this bread, and drink the cup, ye proclaim the Lord's death till he come '), says :

'Here, then, we have the character of the Christian assemblies according to the idea of Him who instituted them ; they are funeral commemorations (*commémoraisons funèbres*) of the Founder. It was He Himself who chose the method, very generally in vogue in His time, the funeral banquet as we have shown, for the purpose of gathering together those who had remained faithful to Him who was among them no more. We would thus have good reasons for seeing here (without eliminating the idea of the Passover in the assemblies described above) a real funeral banquet, comprising a frugal common meal and a sacred repast which was the real object of the meeting together, namely, the receiving of the body and blood of Jesus, "in memory of Him", and "proclaiming His death".'[2]

Against this theory some weighty objections can be urged. Funeral banquets were, of course, 'very generally in vogue' at this time ; Leclercq points, for example, to the practice among the Romans. But, on the supposition that the *Agapé* was a funeral banquet,

[1] *ERE* i. 174 *b*.
[2] In Cabrol's *Dict. d'Arch. Chrét. et de Liturgie*, Fasc. iii. 786 (1903).

is it credible that the Christian rite could have been in imitation of a pagan custom? One has but to remember that at the Roman funeral banquets offerings of food were made to the Manes of the departed [1] to realize that they offer no parallel to the Christian *Agapé*. Equally improbable is the idea that Jewish funeral feasts suggested the institution of the *Agapé*. Leclercq says that towards the end of the first century of our era, thanks to the persistent way in which ancient custom is preserved, the funeral banquet was still found existing among the Jews; and he quotes the well-known expressions 'bread of sorrow' (לֶחֶם אוֹנִים) and 'cup of consolation' (כּוֹס תַּנְחֻמִים), mentioning also in the same connexion Josephus' evidence in *Antiq.* XIV. x. 8 (the decree of Julius Caesar permitting the Jews of Delos to celebrate these banquets). It is perfectly true that funeral feasts, a custom handed down from a hoary antiquity, were in vogue at this time among the Jews; but apart from the fact that these feasts were only held on the occasion of funerals, whereas the *Agapé* was celebrated weekly, it must be remembered that the evidence points to the *Agapé* as being an absolutely primitive Christian custom; this means that the Apostles celebrated it within a few days of the *Resurrection*. Can it be supposed, then, that it was founded on the pattern of a funeral feast? If, as Leclercq holds, the idea of the *Agapé* as a funeral commemoration was that of 'Him who instituted them' (i.e. these Christian assemblies), how does he explain the fact that they were instituted at the Passover Feast? For, according to him, it was a Passover feast at which they took their beginning.

---

[1] See Marquardt. *Das Privatleben der Römer*, p. 380 (1886).

His argument is founded on St. Paul's words : 'For as often as ye eat this bread and drink the cup, ye proclaim the Lord's death till he come'; but one cannot lay stress on 'the Lord's death' to the exclusion of 'till he come', which makes the thought of His death quite different from that ordinarily associated with death. The *Agapé* and the Eucharist were originally connected, the central thought being thanksgiving ; Christ makes no mention of death at the institution ; Mk. xiv. 25 ; Matt. xxvi. 29 ; and Lk. xxii. 18 point, on the contrary, to life.

The most obvious and natural theory of the origin of the *Agapé* is that of those who see in the custom 'an endeavour to follow the precedent of the Last Supper, when the Eucharist was combined with a meal'. The difficulty here is, of course, that the meal is regarded by most as having been a Passover meal ; for the weekly *Agapé* could not well have the annual Passover meal as its pattern.

After what has been said in chap. vi, it will be clear that, according to the theory here advocated, the origin of the *Agapé* is to be found in the common meal which took place weekly immediately before the *Kiddûsh* ceremony which inaugurated the Sabbath.

As already pointed out, these common meals were arranged by groups of friends, and each such group was called a *Chabûrah*. These groups or companies of friends existed for different purposes, into which we need not enter here;[1] but one of these was the weekly meeting referred to. The main idea was that of fellow-

---

[1] See Geiger, *Urschrift* . . ., pp. 122 ff., 179 ; *Tos. Ber.* iv. 19, 20 ; Elbogen, *Op. cit.*, p. 111 ; Abrahams, *Op. cit.*, p. cxl. Interesting details will be found in Büchler, *Der galiläische 'Am-ha' Ares*, pp. 207 ff. (1906).

ship; and though originally the members belonged to the same social grade, this became modified in course of time; and when the common meal, originally, like *Kiddûsh*, a home ceremony, was transferred to the Synagogue, the idea of fellowship was emphasized by the presence of poor as well as rich who partook of it.

The main argument in favour of this theory of the origin of the *Agapé* lies in its obviousness. But there is a further point in its favour, and that is concerned with the name *Agapé*. Keating[1] expresses his belief that the name *Agapé* is derived from Jn. xiii. 34, 'A new commandment I give unto you, that ye love one another' (ἵνα ἀγαπᾶτε ἀλλήλους); but may these words not be an allusion to the name of those groups of friends, one of which was formed by Christ and the Apostles—*Chabûrah*, which means 'fellowship', almost 'love'? The root meaning of this word is a 'bond'; then it comes to mean fellowship among men; and *chabēr* means a 'friend' (cp. Jn. xv. 14, 'Ye are my friends . . .'). It seems, then, to be a fair inference that the name *Agapé* was intended as a Greek equivalent to the neo-Hebrew *Chabûrah*.[2] If so, it strengthens the argument for the theory of the origin of the *Agapé* here advocated.

---

[1] Quoted by Maclean in the article referred to.

[2] The word does not occur in this sense in biblical Hebrew.

IX

THE ORIGIN OF THE EPICLESIS

THE idea of the *Epiclesis* being reckoned among those elements of the Christian Liturgy in which Jewish influence is to be discerned will probably be regarded by many as fantastic. Nevertheless, we contend that it was, in its essence, originally derived from a Jewish conception which was not confined to learned circles, but was also in vogue among the ordinary worshippers in the Synagogue.

In seeking to establish this contention it will be necessary to trace back the history of the *Epiclesis* from the time in which its form is found in the fully developed liturgies of the Eastern Church to its first appearance in Christian literature. There will be no need to cite *all* the documents in which its various forms occur during the periods to be considered;[1] but we shall have to deal briefly with the more important of these.

I

As an example of the *Epiclesis* as found in the eastern liturgy well after the time that this had reached its final state, i. e. during the fifth century, we may take that which occurs in the *Liturgy of St. James* (seventh century). The words which concern us here are as follows :

' Have mercy upon us, Almighty God, have mercy

[1] See Connolly's article in the *Journal of Theological Studies* for July 1924.

upon us, O God our Saviour, have mercy upon us, O God, according to Thy great mercy . . . and send down upon us and upon these holy gifts lying before (Thee) Thine all-holy Spirit, that . . . He may sanctify and make (ἀγιάσῃ καὶ ποιῇ) this bread the holy Body of Christ, and this cup the precious Blood of Christ, that they may be to all who partake of them for the remission of sins and everlasting life, for the sanctification of their souls and bodies . . .' [1]

Two points are to be specially noted here : (1) prayer is offered for the descent of the Spirit upon the worshippers as well as upon the bread and the wine ; (2) the effect of the descent is the sanctification of the worshippers, and the transformation of the elements.

This represents the form and content of the *Epiclesis* from the beginning of the fifth century onwards ; it is unnecessary to give further examples, for by this time the form of the liturgy of the Eastern Church had reached finality.

II

During the fourth century, however, it will be seen that the *Epiclesis* appears in a less-developed form, and that it lacks the uniformity of content which it assumes from the fifth century onwards. Here several examples must be offered.

We take first the *Epiclesis* as it appears in the *Apostolic Constitutions* (Bk. viii), which belongs to the latter part of the fourth century :

'Remembering, therefore, His passion and death and resurrection from the dead and return into heaven, and His future second *Parousia* when He cometh with glory and power to judge the quick and the dead, and to give to each one according to his works,—we offer to Thee, King and God, according to His command,

---

[1] Brightman, *Liturgies Eastern and Western*, i, pp. 53 ff. (1896).

this bread and this cup, giving thanks to Thee through Him because Thou hast made us worthy to stand before Thee and minister as priests to Thee. And we beseech Thee to look graciously on these gifts lying before Thee . . . and to send down Thy Holy Spirit . . . upon this sacrifice . . . that He may shew forth [or "declare", ἀποφήνῃ] this bread the Body of Thy Christ, and this cup the Blood of Thy Christ, that they who partake of it may be strengthened in godliness, may obtain remission of (their) sins, may be delivered from the devil and his deceit, may be filled with the Holy Spirit, may become worthy of Thy Christ, may attain to eternal life, Thou being reconciled to them, O Master Almighty.'[1]

We have here again two elements in the *Epiclesis*: prayer for the descent of the Holy Spirit upon the worshippers for their sanctification, and for His descent upon the bread and wine ; but what is specially noticeable is that the conception of the effect of the Spirit's descent upon these latter is less pronounced than in the case of the fully developed liturgies. The difference between the transforming of the bread and wine ('that He may sanctify and make') in the *Liturgy of St. James*, and the 'shewing forth', or 'declaring', in the *Apostolic Constitutions*, is too obvious to need further comment. In each, what is said about the effect of the Spirit's descent upon the worshippers is, in essence, the same. It is the effect of the Spirit's descent upon the bread and the wine that is conceived of as somewhat different.

To this century belongs the document known as the *Canons of Hippolytus*, derived from the so-called ' Egyptian Church Order'. The relevant passage here runs as follows :

'. . . And we pray Thee that Thou wouldest send

[1] Brightman, *Op. cit.*, i, p. 21.

Thy Holy Spirit upon the oblation of the holy Church; that, joining (them) together in one, Thou wouldest grant to all the holy ones who partake (that it may be to them) for the replenishment of the Holy Spirit unto the strengthening of faith in truth . . .' (*Et petimus ut mittas Spiritum Tuum Sanctum in oblationem sanctae ecclesiae; in unum congregans des omnibus, qui percipiunt, sanctis in repletionem Spiritus Sancti ad confirmationem fidei in veritate . . .*').[1]

It will be noticed that in this form of the *Epiclesis* while prayer is offered for the descent of the Holy Spirit upon the elements ('the oblation of the holy Church'), there is no word about their conversion; the essence of the prayer is for the outpouring of the Holy Spirit upon the partakers.

A further point of importance to note is that in our fourth-century documents it is not always the Third Person of the Holy Trinity whose descent upon the bread and the wine is thought of. Cyril of Jerusalem, for example, who lived during most of the fourth century, writes thus : 'For as the bread and the wine of the Eucharist before the invocation of the holy and adored Trinity were mere bread and wine, when the invocation has taken place the bread becomes the Body of Christ, and the wine the Blood of Christ' (*Catech. Mystag.* i. 7). Elsewhere, however, he speaks of the invocation of the Holy Spirit: '. . . for as the bread of the Eucharist after the invocation of the Holy Spirit (μετὰ τὴν ἐπίκλησιν τοῦ ἁγίου πνεύματος) is no longer mere bread, but the Body of Christ . . .' (*Ibid.* iii. 3). He speaks also of the 'visiting' (ἐπιφοίτησις) of the Holy Spirit which makes the elements holy (*Ibid.* v. 19).

[1] Hauler, *Didascaliae apostolorum fragmenta Veronensia latina,* p. 107 (1900).

In another passage the wording reminds us of the *Liturgy of St. James* just quoted : 'We beseech the merciful God to send forth the Holy Spirit upon the elements set forth, that He may make (ἵνα ποιήσῃ) the bread the Body of Christ, and the wine the Blood of Christ' (*Ibid.* v. 7). In most of his references to the subject Cyril of Jerusalem thus speaks of the invocation of the Holy Spirit ; that he should, in spite of this, speak of the invocation of the Holy Trinity is the more noteworthy.

Different, again, in this respect is the form of the *Epiclesis* in the *Liturgy of Sarapion*, belonging to the middle of the fourth century. This runs : ' O God of truth, may Thy holy Word abide upon this bread, that the bread may become the body of Thy Word ; and upon this cup, that the cup may become the blood of truth.' These words are followed by a prayer for those who are about to partake.[1]

The thought of the Word abiding upon the bread and the cup is very interesting ; and it is important in view of what is to be said later about what we conceive to be the origin of the *Epiclesis*.

We turn next to the *Testament of our Lord*, which belongs also to about the middle of the fourth century:

' Remembering, therefore, Thy death and resurrection, we offer to Thee bread and the cup, giving thanks to Thee who alone art God for ever, and our Saviour, since Thou hast promised to us to stand before Thee and to serve Thee in the priesthood. Therefore we render thanks to Thee, we Thy servants, O Lord . . . We offer to Thee this thanksgiving, Eternal Trinity, O Lord Jesus Christ, O Lord the Father, before whom all creation and every nature trembleth fleeing

[1] Funk, *Didascalia et Constitutiones apostolorum*, ii, pp. 174 ff. (1905).

D d

into itself, O Lord the Holy Ghost; we have brought this drink and this food of Thy holiness [to Thee]; cause that it may be to us not for condemnation, not for reproach, not for destruction, but for the medicine and support of our spirit. Yea, O God, grant us that by Thy Name every thought of things displeasing to Thee may flee away . . . Grant, therefore, O Lord, to our innermost eyes to see Thee, praising Thee and glorifying Thee, commemorating Thee and serving Thee, having a portion in Thee alone, O Son and Word of God, who subduest all things . . . Feed the people in uprightness; sanctify us all, O God; but grant that all those who partake and receive of Thy Holy things may be made one with Thee, so that they may be filled with the Holy Ghost, for the confirmation of the faith in truth . . .' [1]

So far as the fourth-century evidence is concerned there are three points to note: (1) the variation in the form of the *Epiclesis* regarding the Person invoked. In the final stage of liturgical development it is always the third Person of the Holy Trinity who is invoked; but in these fourth-century authorities we find now the Holy Trinity, now the Word, and now the Holy Spirit invoked. It may, therefore, be justifiably inferred that this element in the *Epiclesis* was in a fluid condition during the fourth century. (2) As compared with the definite conception of the conversion of the bread and wine effected by the descent of the Holy Spirit upon them found in the fully developed liturgies, these fourth-century authorities are, with the exception of Cyril of Jerusalem, indefinite. This is especially true of the *Liturgy of Sarapion*, containing as it does the phrases 'the body of Thy Word', 'the blood of truth'. (3) The other element in the *Epiclesis*, the prayer for the worshippers, is always present, whether in the fully

---

[1] Cooper and Maclean, *The Testament of our Lord*, pp. 73 ff. (1902).

developed liturgies of later centuries or in the fourth-century authorities. Cyril, it is true, does not make any mention of this; but this is probably due to the fact that the object of his references to the *Epiclesis* does not call for any mention of this part of it. In v. 3–6 of his *Catecheseis*, where he gives a brief *résumé* of the anaphoral portion of his liturgy, he makes no mention of the Institution itself or of the words of Christ over the bread and the wine ; but we should not deduce from this that they were actually omitted in the prayer of consecration of his liturgy. Since the other fourth-century authorities mention the prayer for the worshippers, and since it occurs in all other authorities, whether after or before the fourth century, it may be regarded as certain that it found a place in the liturgy Cyril used, even though he does not mention it in his account of the liturgy.

It will have been noticed, further, that in the form of the *Epiclesis* which occurs in *The Testament of our Lord* there is no prayer for the descent of the Holy Spirit upon the bread and the wine. In view of the fact that in the *Testament* we have a full and *verbatim* text this omission can scarcely be accidental.

This variability, which seems to have been character-istic of the *Epiclesis* during the fourth century, and which will be seen to be further emphasized by the evidence of the third and second centuries, leads to the conclusion that there was, at any rate in the earlier centuries of Christianity, not the same importance attached to this part of the *Epiclesis* as there was to that part which speaks of the Divine Presence among, and blessing of, the worshippers. In the *Epiclesis* last quoted, prayer for union between God and His wor-shippers, together with the petition that the Holy

Spirit may abide in them, seems to be the essence of it. And this is the part which, in one form or another, is invariable in every *Epiclesis*, whatever the century.

The examples of the fourth-century evidence on the subject which have been offered do not profess to be exhaustive ; but that they fairly represent the form and content of the *Epiclesis*, so far as this century is concerned, will not be denied.

III

Turning now to the third century ; Origen, in his *Homilies on* 1 *Cor.*, commenting on vii. 5, says : ' Then, in order that a man may take the shewbread he must be pure from woman (1 Sam. xxi. 4) ; but in order that he may take the bread which is greater than the shew-bread, (even that) on which has been invoked the name of God, and of Christ, and of the Holy Spirit, ought not a man to be purer by far, so that he may truly take the bread unto salvation and not unto judgement ?' [1] An invocation of the Holy Trinity is clearly referred to here, Origen's evidence thus agreeing with what in one instance, at any rate, Cyril of Jerusalem says. Elsewhere he refers to the other element in the *Epiclesis*, the sanctification of the worshippers. [2]

Coming next to Cyprian, we have no information in his writings about the wording of the *Epiclesis*. He speaks of the bread and wine which Christ offered

---

[1] See Jenkins, in *JTS*, p. 502 (1908).

[2] He speaks of the Body of Christ as ἁγιάζον τοὺς μετὰ ὑγιοῦς προθέσεως αὐτῷ χρωμένους (*Contra Cels.* viii. 53), quoted by Woolley, *Op. cit.*, p. 100. In the same passage Origen speaks of the bread becoming the Body ' through prayer '.

to God the Father as 'His Body and Blood',[1] but makes no mention of the Holy Spirit coming upon them. Elsewhere, however, he says that 'the oblation cannot be sanctified where the Holy Spirit is not';[2] and in another letter he speaks of 'the Lord's sacrifice' as celebrated 'with the appointed sanctification (*legitima sanctificatione*)';[3] this could, conceivably, refer to the *Epiclesis*.

Cyprian nowhere definitely refers to a prayer for the descent of the Holy Spirit upon the worshippers; but nothing can be gathered from the non-mention of this. One passage certainly shows that the sanctification of the communicants was in his mind, for he speaks of the mixed cup of wine and water, and sees in it a symbol of the union of Christ with His people.[4]

The only passage in Tertullian in which there seems to be a reference to the *Epiclesis* is where he says that Christ made the bread His Body by the words of institution, though he explains this as 'the figure' of His Body.[5] If, however, Tertullian did have the *Epiclesis* in mind when writing these words, he clearly knew of no prayer for the descent of the Holy Spirit upon the elements. He does not refer to any prayer for the Holy Spirit to come down upon the worshippers, unless this is included in the *Orationes sacrificiorum* spoken of in his *De Orat.* xiv.

We have seen that the *Acts of Thomas*, belonging in all probability to the second quarter of the third century, though an apocryphal work contains nothing

---

[1] *Ep.* lxiii.   [2] *Ep.* lxv (lxiv).

[3] *Ep.* lxiii. These passages are quoted by Srawley, *Op. cit.*, pp. 138 ff.

[4] *Ep.* lxiii. 13 (Srawley, *Op. cit.*, p. 137).

[5] ... *Acceptum panem et distributum discipulis corpus suum illum fecit 'Hoc est corpus meum' dicendo, id est figura corporis mei* (*Adv. Marc.* iv. 40).

of an unorthodox character; it is, therefore, not un-
reasonable to suppose that references to the *Epiclesis*
which may be discerned reflect the Catholic stand-
point.[1]

The first relevant passage occurs in chaps. xlix, l.
So far as the words in chap. xlix are concerned, the
Syriac form considerably expands what the Greek
has; we give a translation of the latter as probably
nearer the original form : 'Jesu, who hast deemed us
worthy to partake of the eucharist of Thy holy body
and blood, behold, we are bold to draw nigh to Thy
eucharist, and to invoke Thy holy Name; come and
communicate unto us.' There follows then, in chap. l,
an elaborated *Epiclesis*, in which the Syriac and the
Greek differ very considerably; but the main difference
between them (so far as our present inquiry is concerned) is that in the Greek form it is the Holy Spirit
('the holy dove') who is invoked, whereas in the Syriac
the invocation is that of 'the Holy Spirit', the 'power
of the Father', and the 'wisdom of the Son'—'for ye
are One in all'; i.e. it is the invocation of the Holy
Trinity.

The next passage is in chap. cxxxiii, where again
the Syriac and the Greek differ widely. According to
the Syriac it is the Holy Trinity which is invoked, and
there is a prayer for the divine blessing upon the
faithful worshippers that their souls may be renewed
and their sins forgiven them. But the Greek has :
'We invoke upon thee ($\epsilon\pi\iota\phi\eta\mu\iota\zeta o\mu\epsilon\nu$ $\sigma\epsilon$, i. e. 'the Bread

---

[1] Most authorities hold that this work was originally written in
Syriac; James, however, believes 'the Acts *were* composed in Greek,
and early rendered into Syriac. Becoming scarce, or being wholly
lost, in Greek, they were retranslated out of Syriac into Greek' (*The
Apocryphal New Testament*, p. 364).

of life ') the name of the mother,[1] of the unspeakable mystery of the hidden powers and authorities; we invoke upon thee the name of Jesus. And he said: Let the powers of blessing come, and be established in this bread, that all the souls which partake of it may be washed from their sins.'

The last passage, which occurs in chap. clviii, does not differ so much in the Syriac and Greek forms. There is no petition for any Person of the Holy Trinity to come down upon the elements; it is an *Epiclesis* which is almost wholly made up of a prayer for the worshippers; the Passion of Christ, with the blessings it confers upon the faithful, forms the essence of it.

These few examples, and they are, we think, fairly exhaustive, of the third-century evidence regarding the *Epiclesis*, emphasize the variability as to the Person of the Holy Trinity invoked which we saw to be the case in the fourth-century evidence. There is also the unvarying element—the prayer for the worshippers— which is characteristic of both centuries.

IV

Finally, we come to the second century.

Irenaeus, in an important passage,[2] speaks of the bread 'receiving the invocation of God', after which it is 'no more common bread, but Eucharist'; and he goes on to show the benefits imparted to man through the Eucharist. He uses the word *Epiclesis*, but not in

---

[1] A Syriac form must lie behind this, because the reference is to the Holy Spirit, 'which in old Syriac is invariably treated as feminine' (Burkitt, in James, *Op. cit.*, p. 378).

[2] *Adv. Haereses*, IV. xviii. 5, xxxi. 4.

its later technical sense; with him it is more or less equivalent to 'prayer'.[1] The idea of the descent of the Holy Spirit on the bread and wine is quite foreign to him.[2]

The apocryphal *Acts of John* belongs approximately to this period; in the account of the Eucharist there is reference to a prayer that the worshippers may be worthy of the grace of the Lord; but no mention whatsoever of prayer for the descent of the Holy Spirit upon the elements.

Justin Martyr makes it quite clear in one passage that the *Epiclesis* was a prayer on behalf of the worshippers.[3] Another passage runs : 'As through the word of God Jesus Christ our Saviour was incarnate, and took flesh and blood for our salvation, so also we have been taught that the food over which thanks have been given through the prayer of the word (or 'word of prayer'; δι' εὐχῆς λόγου) which is from Him (τοῦ παρ' αὐτοῦ), by which food our blood and flesh are nourished by assimilation, is the flesh and blood of that Jesus who became incarnate.'[4] There is some uncertainty as to the meaning of the phrase 'through the prayer of the word'; it may refer to the *Logos*, an interpretation which, as Srawley says, would have 'the advantage of bringing out the parallelism between the operative power of the *Logos* in the Incarnation and in the Eucharist, which is suggested by Justin's

---

[1] Cp. Woolley, *Op. cit.*, p. 72.

[2] He speaks (**I.** vii. 2) of the Gnostic Marcus consecrating the mixed cup by the invocation of the Divine Name; but nowhere mentions the Holy Spirit in this connexion.

[3] . . . ἀναπέμπει καὶ εὐχαριστίαν ὑπὲρ τοῦ κατηξιῶσθαι τούτων παρ' αὐτοῦ ἐπὶ πολὺ ποιεῖται (*Apol.* i. 65).

[4] *Apol.* i. 66.

language'.[1] On the other hand, 'through the word of prayer which is from Him' might quite conceivably refer to the Lord's Prayer, though it is realized that evidence for this use of the Lord's Prayer in this early period is wanting. At any rate, it is clear that Justin is quite unconscious of any idea of prayer being offered for the descent of the Holy Spirit upon the elements; but he speaks directly of the effect of reception upon the worshippers.

The *Didaché* throws no light upon the subject. It is, however, quite possible, as Woolley suggests,[2] that there is an implicit reference to the *Epiclesis* in Ignatius' *Epistle to the Ephesians*, xx: '. . . breaking one bread, which is the medicine of immortality, the antidote that we should not die, but live for ever in Jesus Christ'; for this recalls what Irenaeus says about the bread which has received 'the invocation of God', and the benefits conferred thereby upon the recipients, especially life to body and soul, and the hope of resurrection (*Adv. Haer.* IV. xviii. 5, referred to above).

Thus, while it must be confessed that the information of the second century regarding our subject leaves much to be desired, two points are clear enough: (1) the *Epiclesis* (using a name which as a technical term belongs, of course, to later centuries) contained no petition for the descent of the Holy Spirit upon the bread and wine; and (2) it was concerned, above all, with prayer for the worshippers. So that it may be reasonably maintained that from the beginning what

---

[1] *Op. cit.*, p. 36; cp. Gregory of Nyssa's words when speaking of the bread of the Eucharist as 'sanctified by the Word of God and prayer' (*Or. Cat.* 37, quoted by Srawley, *Op. cit.*, p. 120).

[2] *Op. cit.*, p. 96.

was later known as the *Epiclesis* was in its essence a prayer for the Divine Presence among the worshippers during their most solemn act of worship.

V

Before we come to deal with the subject of what we conceive to have been the origin of the *Epiclesis*, it may be well to say here that we are well aware of the fact that some among leading liturgiological scholars believe that the original conception of the *Epiclesis* is to be found in the Scriptural passages which tell of our Lord's miraculous birth through the operation of the Holy Spirit (Matt. i. 18–20; Lk. i. 35); for they point to the parallel of the Incarnation ('the Holy Ghost shall come upon thee . . . wherefore also that which is to be born shall be called holy . . .' Lk. i. 35) and the Eucharist in which the change in the elements is effected by the descent of the Holy Spirit upon them—at any rate, according to the *Epiclesis* in its more developed form. Passages from the Church Fathers are cited in support of this.[1] There are, however, two objections which are fatal to this theory of the origin of the *Epiclesis*. One is that it is not borne out by the evidence; we have seen that during the first three centuries of the history of the *Epiclesis* there is no mention in it of the change in the elements being effected by the descent of the Holy Spirit upon them. The force of the theory would be immensely strengthened if the evidence of these first three centuries could be eliminated. There is also the fact that even after the third century it is not always the Third

[1] Renaudot, *Liturgiarum orientalium collectio*, ii, pp. 512ff. (1711); Salaville, *Les fondements scripturaires de l'épiclèse*, in *Échos d'Orient*, pp. 5 ff. (1909).

Person whose descent is asked for in the *Epiclesis* prayer.

The other objection is even stronger; it is that the Eucharistic doctrine involved is too developed for the first three centuries. This is not the place to enter upon the details of this subject; but it is certain that the evidence of the writers of this period does not point to the development of doctrine postulated by the theory.

It is more natural, we maintain, to look for a simpler explanation of the origin of the *Epiclesis*; for this is more in accordance with the informal and simple character in general of the doctrine and thought and practice of the primitive Church. A prayer for the Divine Presence among the assembled worshippers during their most solemn act of worship; this, as we have already said, we conceive to have been the original form of what ultimately developed into the *Epiclesis*. 'Where two or three are gathered together in my name, there am I in the midst of them' (Matt. xviii. 20).

It can scarcely be doubted that in the first instance that presence must have been in reference to any informal gathering for worship, no matter how small the number of worshippers. The thought of Christ's presence in spirit would then have been equally in the mind of the early Jewish-Christians when they assembled for their accustomed worship in the Temple or in the Synagogue. Still more would it have been the case, later, when they gathered together on the first day of the week for the breaking of bread.

The question then arises as to whether, in earlier Jewish belief, there were any antecedent conceptions which formed the seed-field from which this belief in and conviction of the Divine Presence developed. We venture to think that in answer to this question there were three conceptions, rooted in Judaism, all of which played their part here; but that one in particular must be regarded as the immediate parent of the conception contained in the *Epiclesis* in its original form.

i. The first of these has been very clearly set forth by Dean Armitage Robinson,[1] namely the Jewish practice of calling the Divine Name over places and persons.[2] In both the Jewish and early Christian Church ' the secret of the Divine Name was kept from those who knew it not already. It was the power inherent in the Name that occasioned this caution; and a parallel is found to it in the anxiety which some early Church writers display that the sacred elements of the Eucharist should be jealously guarded.' Then, after referring to a striking passage of Origen in the *Philocalia* (cap. xvii; from *Contra Celsum*), he continues:

' This preliminary observation enables us to understand the importance attached to the hallowing of places or of persons by putting the Divine Name upon them. "This house whereupon my Name is called" [3] comes again and again in the book of Jeremiah (vii. 10 f., 14). "Thou, O Lord", cries the same prophet, "art in the midst of us and thy Name hath been called upon us: leave us not" (xiv. 9). On His temple and on His people the hallowing Name has been invoked (ἐπικέκληται). The Greek for this naming or invoking means first of all merely "name", or sometimes to

[1] In *Theology*, February No., 1924, pp. 89 ff.

[2] ' The power of the Divine Name was a central conception of Hebrew religion.'

[3] More accurately, ' *over* which my Name is called ', for the idea of contact is not included; the phrase simply denotes ownership.

" surname " (ἐπικαλεῖν) : presently (especially in the middle voice, ἐπικαλεῖσθαι) it gets the meaning to " appeal by name ". It is thus used in adjuration (calling to witness) and imprecation, and so in the general sense of invocation. Hence it is an accompaniment of prayer.'

This is exceedingly suggestive, and the facts here pointed out must have played a part in the history of the origin of the *Epiclesis*. But we venture to think, for reasons to be referred to presently, that this idea of calling the Divine Name over things was subsidiary, not the central conception from which the *Epiclesis* was developed.

ii. Another thing which, in all probability, contributed to this development is concerned with the central event of Christ's Baptism, the outpouring of the Holy Spirit upon Him. For we have something here which offers an analogy to the descent of the Holy Spirit upon the Eucharistic elements prayed for in the more developed form of the *Epiclesis*. How in quite early times Jewish-Christians conceived of the outpouring of the Holy Spirit on Christ at His Baptism is well reflected in the second-century *Gospel of the Nazarenes* : ' It came to pass, when the Lord had come up from the water, that the entire fountain of the Holy Spirit descended and rested upon Him, and said to Him, My Son, in all the prophets I was looking for Thee, that Thou mightest come, and that I might rest in Thee ; for Thou art my rest ; Thou art my first-born Son that reignest for ever ' (Jerome, *Comm. in Isa.* iv. 156). ' The entire fountain of the Holy Spirit ' is a remarkable expression, says Dr. A. F. Findlay,[1] in commenting on this passage ; he thinks the

---

[1] *Byways in Early Christian Literature*, p. 71 (1923).

metaphor was probably suggested by such a passage as 'I will pour out my spirit upon all flesh' (Joel ii. 28) ; and he continues :

' It is manifest that this account of our Lord's experience at Baptism is strongly influenced by the Old Testament, which is precisely what one might expect in a Gospel used by Jewish-Christians with orthodox sympathies. Among Christians of that type there was a deep sense of the unity of the Church with the Old Testament *ecclesia* to which the Divine promises had been given, and central in their thoughts of Jesus was the faith that He was the Messiah in whom the ancient prophecies had been fulfilled. The connexion of this baptismal fragment with Old Testament prophecy is unmistakable. It was quoted by Jerome when he was commenting on Isa. xi. 2 : " the spirit of the Lord shall rest upon him ", and there is no room for doubt that the representation of the Nazarene Gospel was based on these words and on the further conception, which had its roots in Judaism, that the Divine Spirit, which was partially manifested in the prophets, would be completely revealed in the Messiah. . . .'

If the conception expressed in the passage from the Nazarene Gospel was at all widespread in the early Church—and Jerome's use of it would suggest that this was the case—it is quite possible that it may have contributed something towards the idea of the descent of the Holy Spirit upon the sacred Eucharistic elements. The same could, of course, be said of the Synoptic accounts of the Baptism, though these have not the significant development contained in the words of the Nazarene Gospel: '. . . that I might rest in Thee ; for Thou art my rest' (*ut . . . requiescerem in te. Tu es enim requies mea*).

The calling of the Divine Name over things and persons, which was customary both in the Jewish

Church and among the early Christian communities, and the conception of the outpouring of the Holy Spirit on Christ at His Baptism and resting in Him, must certainly be regarded as having had a place in the history of the development of the *Epiclesis*. But in regard to the former, there are two reasons why, as we believe, it can only have been indirectly contributary: (1) the essence of the idea is that of calling the Divine Name *over* things and persons; there is no thought of 'contact' such as was conceived of when it was believed that the Holy Spirit descended upon the worshippers at the Eucharist and abode in them, or when He came down upon the elements to transform them into the Body and Blood. (2) And further, although the Divine Name may have come near to being regarded as an hypostasis, this is a very different thing from the Divine Person. The idea of uttering the Divine Name over things or persons is inadequate and too external in its nature to constitute a *direct* antecedent of the *Epiclesis* conceptions.

As to the latter, there lies behind it precisely the same conception as that which we believe to have been the real antecedent of the *Epiclesis*, and of which we have an illustration in the account of the Transfiguration: '. . . while he was yet speaking, behold, a bright cloud overshadowed them' (νεφέλη φωτεινὴ ἐπεσκίασεν αὐτούς); therefore, while it may well be regarded as having a place in the history of the ideas which culminated in the *Epiclesis*, it did not in itself contribute to this development.

iii. We come, then, to a third conception, rooted in Judaism, which to both Jews and Jewish-Christians was thoroughly familiar, and which we believe to have been the immediate antecedent of the *Epiclesis*; we mean the conception of the divine *Shekhinah*.

This word comes from the Hebrew root *shakan*, which means ' to dwell' or ' abide upon'. The origin of the *Shekhinah* in its technical sense is to be found in such Old Testament passages as Exod. xl. 34 ff., in which we are told that the 'glory of the Lord filled the tabernacle' (*mishkan*, also from the root *shakan*). The glory of the Lord, conceived of as a bright shining cloud, was the sign of the Divine Presence. Thus the ideas of God's 'glory' and of His 'indwelling' were closely associated.[1] But the word came to be used very frequently of the divine 'indwelling' or 'abiding upon' in an invisible way quite apart from any visible glory. For example, in the *Targum of Onkelos* to Deut. xii. 5, and elsewhere, the Temple, as pre-eminently the place of worship, is called ' the house of the *Shekhinah*'; and while there is no idea of a visible presence the thought of the divine abiding upon or indwelling among the worshippers there is none the less present. In the Mishnah, *Aboth* iii. 3, a saying is preserved by Rabbi Chananiah ben Teradyon, who lived in the second half of the first century and early part of the second century, to this effect : 'Where two sit together and are occupied with the words of the Torah, there is the *Shekhinah* among them.' It need hardly be pointed out that to the Jews of that period the study of the Law was regarded as that which was most acceptable in the sight of God, and in a real sense an act of worship. The words quoted recall at once Matt. xviii. 20: ' Where two or three are gathered together in my name, there am I in the midst of them.'

[1] See further on this, Abelson's *The Immanence of God in Rabbinical Literature*, pp. 380 ff. (1912).

In his admirable work *The Immanence of God in Rabbinical Literature*, Dr. Abelson deals fully with the doctrine of the *Shekhinah*, and shows the relationship between the *Shekhinah* and the *Memra* (the ' Word ') and the Holy Spirit respectively. He brings out clearly by many quotations the place that belief in the *Shekhinah* had in early Judaism. This doctrine was one of the ways whereby the immanence of God was taught. In one passage which, though comparatively late,[1] reflects earlier ideas, God and *Shekhinah* are interchangeable terms ; this is in accordance with Rabbinic usage. In his chapter on the personified *Shekhinah* as the immanent God in Palestine, the Temple, and the Synagogue, Dr. Abelson says : ' It is only to be expected that the immanent God of the universe should, in the minds of the Rabbins, be in an even truer and more emphatic sense, the immanent God of the Holy Land. And that God should be immanent in Temple and Synagogue, is a doctrine the foundation of which is seen in nearly all the more familiar passages of the Bible and the Jewish Prayer-Book.'[2] And he illustrates this by various quotations from Rabbinical literature.

We have, then, in this conception of the *Shekhinah* one with which the Jews were thoroughly familiar at the beginning of the Christian era, and which expressed the belief in a divine presence among those gathered together in the name of God for worship. We say that the Jews were thoroughly familiar with this idea ; for it might be thought that a conception of this kind would be confined to learned circles, and not shared by the ordinary worshippers among the common people. But this was not so. The fact is that this

---

[1] In the Introduction to *Ekah* (*Lamentations*) *Rabba*.   [2] p. 117.

word *Shekhinah* occurs more frequently in those explanatory versions of the Scriptures, the Targums, which were read, and often further commented on, in the synagogue worship for the benefit of the common people, than anywhere else in ancient Jewish literature. 'The word *Shekhinah*', says Ludwig Blau,[1] 'occurs most frequently in the Aramaic Versions, since they were intended for the people, and were actually read to them, and since precautions had therefore to be taken against possible misunderstandings in regard to the conception of God.'

It is impossible to believe that a popular belief such as this, which made a very natural appeal to worshippers of all classes, should have been without its influence on the first Jewish-Christians. While in the first instance the Divine Presence would be thought of and expressed as that of the Heavenly Father, a modified mode of expression would have arisen as a result of the experience at Pentecost; and this transition would have been the easier if, as is most probably the case, the not infrequent Talmudical explanation of the *Shekhinah* as the Holy Spirit of God, reflects earlier thought.

And then we have a further consideration which is so clearly expressed by Taylor that we cannot do better than quote his words:

'*Shekhinah* is sometimes practically equivalent to *Memra* (*Logos*), but one may distinguish between them by regarding the one as the medium of a *passive*, the other of an *active* manifestation; the one as creative, the other as overshadowing or indwelling. The two are brought together by St. John, in whose theology the conceptions assume a new definiteness, and the medium becomes a Mediator: *The Word was made*

[1] *JE* xi. 259 *a*.

flesh and dwelt (ἐσκήνωσεν) *among us* (i. 14). The word σκηνή and its derivatives are chosen on account of their assonance with the Hebrew to express the *Shekhinah* and its dwelling with men; cp. especially Rev. xxi. 3 (*Behold, the tabernacle of God is with men, and he shall tabernacle with them, and they shall be his peoples, and God Himself shall be with them*); and, indeed, so closely does *Shekhinah* resemble σκηνή that the former has even been thought of as a transliteration of the other.'[1]

We have here, then, some ideas which may well be regarded as throwing light on the origin of the *Epiclesis*. There is the thought of God 'tabernacling' among His people through the descent of the *Shekhinah*, or Divine Presence. Though this was conceived of as a visible presence in days gone by, there is no sort of doubt that at the period of which we are thinking (the earliest days of Christianity) and for long before, this presence was believed to be none the less real for being invisible. Then we have the identification of the Spirit of God with the *Shekhinah*; not, of course, in the developed Christian sense, but nevertheless a belief in the real presence of God by His Spirit. The experience of the first Jewish-Christians at Pentecost gave this a new and fuller meaning. Further, there was the thought of the *Shekhinah* and the *Memra* ('Word' of God) being one and the same. Just as the Jews thought of the *Shekhinah* as the Word of God influencing men by its indwelling, so in the early days of Christianity a fuller conception taught that 'the Word was made flesh and dwelt among' men.[2]

[1] *Sayings of the Jewish Fathers*, p. 44 (1897).

[2] The identity of the *Shekhinah* with the *Memra* is clearly reflected in the words: 'we beheld his *glory*, the glory as of the only begotten from the Father'; cp. also 2 Cor. xii. 9: '. . . that the power of Christ may rest upon me' (ἐπισκηνώσῃ ἐπ' ἐμέ).

The essence of these thoughts was the truth of the divine indwelling, expressed in different ways with the object of making it real to believers; and it was in the natural order of things to conceive of this Divine Presence and indwelling as taking place primarily during gatherings for worship.

The first Christians grew up within a religious atmosphere in which these beliefs regarding the Divine Presence were as natural as the air they breathed; so that the influence of them is more than likely to have asserted itself when specifically Christian worship on the first day of the week took place; and this influence is to be seen, we contend, in the prayer which, in course of time, came to be known as the *Epiclesis*, a prayer which there is every reason to believe existed in some form from the very beginning of Christian worship.

VI

In the brief review which we took of the history of the *Epiclesis*, working backwards from the time of its full development to the earliest notices of it which we possess, two or three facts regarding it emerge quite clearly :

i. The first is that in one form or another the *Epiclesis* has been an element in the Eucharistic worship of the Church from the earliest times. This means, of course, that it was in use among Jews who had become Christians (not that they were differentiated in the earliest age) from the time that specifically Christian worship first began. The conception of the *Shekhinah*, familiar as it was to all Jews, would have been the obvious one to suggest a prayer for the sanctification of the worshippers, gathered together in the Name of God, by means of the descent of the Divine Spirit upon them. The truth contained in the words of Christ: ' Where two or three are gathered together in my name, there am I in the midst of them ', were thought of as taking place in the way that He Himself indicated : ' I will pray the Father, and he shall give you another Comforter, that he may be with you for ever, even the Spirit of truth . . . ye know him ; for he abideth with you, and shall be in you ' (Jn. xiv. 16, 17, cp. 26).

ii. The second fact which comes out so clearly as not to admit of dispute is that in its earliest form the *Epiclesis* consisted solely of prayer for the descent of the Holy Spirit (or of the Word, or of the Holy Trinity) upon the assembled worshippers. There was at first no thought of the bread and wine becoming the Body and Blood of Christ through the operation of the Holy Spirit. That truth was accepted without any attempt to explain how it was brought about. But the content of the simpler and more primitive form of the *Epiclesis* prayer is essentially Jewish; and the *Shekhinah* conception, teaching the truth of the Divine Presence among worshippers, is precisely that which prompts it. The conclusion seems, therefore, irresistible that the origin of the *Epiclesis* is to be sought in the Jewish conception of the *Shekhinah*.

iii. A further fact, which may perhaps be significant, is that it is not always the Holy Spirit for whose descent (whether upon the worshippers or upon the elements) prayer is offered. We have seen from the examples given that during the period of the second, third, and fourth centuries it is either the Holy Spirit, or the Word, or the Holy Trinity, whose presence is prayed for, though upon the whole the first predominates. These variations may, of course, be due to the simple fact that in these early centuries a fixed form of service had not yet been formulated. On the other hand they may be due to the fact, already pointed out, that in Jewish belief the Holy Spirit on the one hand, and the *Memra* [1] ('Word') on the other, are identified with the *Shekhinah*. If, as we hold, the *Shekhinah* conception gave birth to the *Epiclesis* prayer in its primitive form, it is easy to understand why this latter should exhibit the variations indicated.

Our contention, then, as to the origin of the *Epiclesis* points to a further instance of Jewish influence on early forms of Christian worship.

[1] For which the term *Dibbur* (less frequently *Ma'amar*) is used; but the connotation is the same.

INDEXES

I. SUBJECTS

II. BIBLICAL REFERENCES

III. ANCIENT AUTHORS AND ANCIENT WRITINGS

IV. REFERENCES TO RABBINICAL LITERATURE

V. MODERN AUTHORS

PRINTED IN ENGLAND
AT THE OXFORD UNIVERSITY PRESS